I Never Knew That About

OURAY

BY P. DAVID SMITH

WESTERN REFLECTIONS PUBLISHING COMPANY®

Lake City, Colorado

ISBN 978-1-937851-52-1

First Edition
Printed in the United States of America

Cover and Text Design by Laurie Casselberry
Laurie Goralka Design

Western Reflections Publishing Company
P. O. Box 1149
951B North Highway 149
Lake City, Colorado 81235
www.westernreflectionspublishing.com
(970) 944-0110

This book is dedicated to Jack and Doris Swanson, who encouraged me to write my first book forty years ago and who gave me the knowledge of what a good book should look like and what a publisher should do for himself, his authors, and his bookstores. Thank you Jack and Doris.

We miss you.

Table of Contents

～ ～

INTRODUCTION
The City of Ouray

~ ~

The City of Ouray nestles cozily in its mountain bowl near the northwest corner of the San Juan Mountains of southwestern Colorado. Its natural beauty and grandeur have always attracted many admirers. Even as early as 1885 travel writer Ernest Ingersoll was impressed enough to write in *Crest of the Continent:*

> *Ouray is – what shall I say? The prettiest mountain town in Colorado? That wouldn't do. A dozen other places would deny it.... Yet that it is among the most attractive in situation, in climate, in appearance, and in the society it affords, there can be no doubt. There are few western villages that can boast of so much civilization.*

It is said that a child who is loved has many names, and the City of Ouray is no exception. Among other monikers it has been called "Uncompahgre City," "Gem of the Rockies," "Opal of the Rockies," "The Switzerland of America," and "God's Country." If the town is the gem, then the bowl that the town sits in must be a platinum setting. The bowl is not, as many new visitors think, part of a volcanic eruption. Rather it was carved by glaciers about a million years ago. This particular mass of ice was relatively small but was joined by two large glaciers that slowly moved down the Uncompahgre River and Canyon Creek tens of thousands of years ago. The melting ice of the glaciers made the rivers and creeks run much higher that they do today. It is also a good bet that over the eons other glaciers slid through the canyon, making the bowl less deep on west and north sides. The freezing and thawing of the glaciers cracked the surrounding rock and carved out bowls (called cirques), of which the amphitheater is a classic example.

There is just something about Ouray – this writer would describe it as extremely "cozy." It's a place where one can sit or lay back and feel comfortable, whether in the hot springs pool or on a motel room porch looking at the surrounding mountains and cliffs. Ouray is a place for a family to get to know each other again, a place to relax and let those little worries slip away. Ouray is a town in which to slow down enough to enjoy nature's beauty and find inspiration in the little glories of life. Enjoy the colors of the cliffs, the sound of the creeks and waterfalls, the sight of an alpenglow outlined Cleopatra in red at the upper middle top edge of the amphitheater, or the touch of the spray from any of Ouray's three large and many small waterfalls. Some of its appeal is its history, some of it is "secret" spots or unexpected places, and some of it is the intangible spirit of the people who have and do live here.

The first visitors to Ouray's bowl were probably Paleo Indians, who arrived in what is now Western Colorado as early as 12,000 years ago. It would have looked very different as small remnants of glaciers would have been present and the flora and fauna would have been different because of a wetter and warmer climate. The Paleo were followed by the Archaic Indians, who used atlatyls (throwing stick for small spears or darts) to hunt, and by 1,000 A.D. the Anasazi and Fremont were using bow and arrows to hunt the plentiful game in Ouray's amphitheater. However this book begins with recorded history, the first being the Escalante and Dominguez expedition of 1776, Spaniards who passed through today's Ouray County near the future Ridgway and Colona. There have been a few artifacts found that indicate that other Spanish visitors were in the Ouray area at a later time, but we have no written record of their activities.

Ouray was first settled by Whites in 1875, although it was known by them to be a good spot for a town since 1860 or earlier. It had been used as a camping spot by the Utes Indians for centuries, as it had good game and firewood (it was heavily wooded then), good water for drinking, and healing hot springs that were a major attraction. The first name chosen for the town was Uncompahgre, but it was soon changed to Ouray in an effort of goodwill toward the nearby Utes. The river was already called "Uncompahgre," a Ute word meaning "red, hot springs." Chief Ouray was a good friend of the Whites. The Americans considered the Utes the smartest of all the western Native American tribes and the Tabeguache (which was the Ute band nearest the new town of Ouray) was the largest and considered the smartest of the seven Utes bands, probably because of the knowledge they gained through their century's long contact with the Spanish before the Americans arrived. Chief Ouray was considered by the Whites to be the smartest of the Tabeguache.

At the time (1875) that the small settlement of Ouray was being started, the Tabeguache Ute Agency was being moved from Cochetopa Pass to the Uncompahgre River Valley near today's Colona. The Utes were not happy about the Whites pouring into Western Colorado and the San Juans and despite previous treaties, an uprising was very possible among the majority of Utes. By 1875, the Utes had already made four treaties with the Americans. The first treaty was in 1849 in which the Utes simply promised to stay in their traditional territory and remain friendly; the second was in 1863 but was later declared null and void when U. S. legislators changed the wording without Ute permission or even knowledge; the third was in 1868 (when the Utes were recognized as owning all the land in Colorado that was basically west of the Continental Divide (the Utes at the time had no real concept of land ownership); and then in the Treaty of 1873 (when the U. S. bought the San Juan Mountains from the Utes), the Ouray bowl was in American territory for the first time. The treaty that removed the Tabeguache Utes from Colorado was made in 1881.

A few American prospectors came to the Ouray bowl in 1860 (when it was still very much Ute territory) and left a written record in the form of a diary, and American mountain men must certainly have passed through the site in the 1820s or 1830s, although the Ute Indians didn't cede the San Juans to the United States until 1873 (but the treaty wasn't ratified by the U. S. until 1874). Milton Cline, Judge Long and brothers Shaff and William Cutler drove a team and wagon to Del Norte in October to get supplies for the winter. Begole and Eckles also made several trips back to civilization that winter to take ore to the smelters and bring back supplies. They originally came over the mountains from Howardsville in Baker's Park, near where Silverton is now situated, but later trips were probably made alongside the Gunnison River and over Cochetopa Pass.. They filed on the Cedar and Clipper lodes at the edge of the town site and kept prospecting as much as possible during the winter. Only a dozen or so men spent that first winter in the Ouray bowl.

By January 1877 Ouray had been named the county seat of Ouray County (it was part of San Juan County before then), and Ouray County was much bigger than the present county. The prospectors were to find a large number of mineral rich veins near Ouray, but the San

This 1877 pen and ink drawing is one of the earliest known representations of Ouray. The artist "cleaned up the town a little. For example a photo taken the next year show plenty of tree stumps in the streets. The commercial district in Main Street is starting to develop and the giant (13 by 20 foot) flag can be seen on its fifty foot flag pole. (Author's Collection)

Juan Mountains also greatly impressed the awe-struck miners with its scenery. Within thirty-five miles of the new town of Ouray were ten peaks that were 14,000 feet in elevation or higher. Several 13,000 foot mountains can be seen from within Ouray's city limits. Five creeks or rivers run through the town site, creating three big, beautiful waterfalls in or near the area. Odorless hot water arose in many different spots, just beckoning the prospectors to bathe and relax in the hot waters. Early travel writers and photographers, such as William H. Jackson and Ernest Ingersol began to capture and sing the praises of Ouray. Travel writer George Crofutt, in his 1885 *Grip-Sack Guide to Colorado*, wrote:

> *The little park in which (Ouray) is situated is nearly round, and about one-fourth mile in diameter* (it's bigger than that, but the "cozy factor" was in play). *On all sides the canyon walls and mountains rise, range after range, peak overshadowing peak, all grooved*

and furrowed by the hand of the Great Maker... In the grand
center of this great circle, the grand amphitheater of nature, com-
pared with which the Coliseum of Rome was an infant, lies the
City of Ouray.

Unlike many of the still existing Colorado mining towns, Ouray was a tourist attraction almost from its founding because of its beautiful location and surroundings. Yet there was also the reason the prospectors came in the first place – the mountains that surround Ouray were and still are some of the most highly mineralized in all of Colorado.

There has been plenty of history created in Ouray County since that time, but this book will only focus on a few highlights, mostly unknown to the general reader, but many well known to local historians. This is not meant to be a book of trivia, although a few of the incidents might be considered such. It is a book of long forgotten or little-publicized facts, but all are interesting information about people, places, and events.

Ouray was pretty well developed by 1885. To the left of the photo was its fire house with a hose cart sitting out front. The building also served as city hall. A log cabin back by the alley served as a jail. To the right is the fifty foot flagpole.   (Author's Collection)

A Few Facts

The City of Ouray's elevation is 7,770 to 7,792 feet depending on where the measurement is taken in town.

There is an average of 285 days a year in which the sun shines at least part of the day in Ouray.

Summer temperatures range from the 50s at night to the 80s in the afternoon.

Winter temperatures run between the teens and the 40s.

Ouray's humidity is very low making it necessary to drink lots of water.

There is an average of 140 inches of snow in Ouray each winter, but it can snow 40 inches or more in 24 hours.

The new city had been laid out, named "Uncompahgre City," and platted in 1875 by A. W. "Gus" Begole and John Eckles. However a new group of arrivals in the spring of 1876 did not like the original town fathers and decided to form a new town at the same spot with different officers. There was almost a war between these two groups of Whites but the second group won out and decided that naming the town "Ouray" might help keep the Utes peaceful. The federal government was paid $375 for the site. The Town of Ouray was officially incorporated in the fall of 1876 and had 400 residents by that time.

Canyon Creek and Box Canyon both used the Spanish spelling of "cañon" for years after Ouray's discovery. Later the spelling was "modernized" to "canyon." Now there seems to be a trend to go back to the original spelling.

Ouray County encompasses 542 square miles and its elevation ranges from the peak of 14,150 feet at Mt. Sneffels down to 6,384 feet on the Uncompahgre River at Colona at the northern county boundary.

Ouray County's population is about 4,794 (2017) and that of the City of Ouray about 1,013 (2017).

Ouray is called a "city" because at one time in 1884 it met the population standard of a city. Although it has been nowhere close to that for many years it has been allowed to keep the designation of "city." Colorado law makes very few distinctions at present between a city and a town.

At one time there were thirty major mines operating in Ouray County. Today there are no major mines, although there are several, like the Idarado that have skeleton crews keeping the mines open if mineral values rise high enough. There are also a few small mines operating (two to six workers). Ouray County still has plenty of minerals to mine.

One reason that Ouray looks so "cozy" is that about two-thirds of its original Victorian homes and commercial buildings still stand, as Ouray, as opposed to almost all western mining towns, has never had a major fire.

Ouray was formed from San Juan County on March 7, 1877. At its formation Ouray County also included what is today San Miguel and Delores Counties. The first county courthouse was built by Sheriff Jess Benton and was called "Benton Hall," with the county records being kept on the second floor.

People

ALFRED CASTNER KING
Blind Poet of the San Juans

A mong some of the most amazing accomplishments of the many prospectors, mining men, and brave women of the San Juan Mountains are those of a former miner and prospector – Alfred Castner King – who, of all things, became famous in literary circles throughout Colorado, the United States, and the world for his poetry. King eventually authored two well-received books, traveled the literary circuit in Europe and the U. S., and made a reasonable living reciting his poetry to entranced audiences that often numbered in the many hundreds. Some of his poems were dozens or even hundreds of pages long and many centered on the incredible beauty (but hard to describe in prose) of the San Juan Mountains. All of his recitations were from memory, as Alfred was totally blind after he was injured in a mining accident before he began his career as a poet.

King was born in Leslie, Michigan, in 1873. His

Alfred Castner King was not handicapped by his blindness and traveled all over the world reciting his poetry. He even signed his books, although it made it obvious he was blind.

(Author's Collection)

father died when Alfred
was only three, and his
mother eventually moved
with him to Colorado,
remarried, and ended up in the booming mining town of Ouray. Alfred
was only eight at this time but was already writing poetry with the
encouragement of his mother. King became a miner in the mid-1890s to
help with the family's finances. King related in his first book, *Mountain
Idylls and Other Poems*:

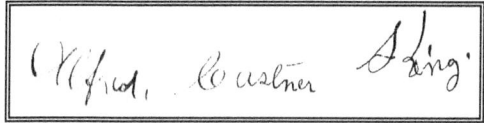

> *On the 17th of March, A.D. 1900, occurred an accident in the
> form of a premature mining explosion, which banished the light of
> the Colorado sun from (my eyes) forever, adding the almost insur-
> mountable barrier of total and helpless blindness to those of limited
> means and insufficient education.*

The *Ouray Herald* of March 22, 1900 gives us further details:

> *He was capping a fuse when not more than 3 or 4 feet from him
> were piled a number of boxes of giant caps (primers). For some
> unaccountable manner, three of these cases exploded and flying
> missiles struck the unfortunate man in the face and arms and body.*

King was taken to Denver where he was seen by "one of the state's
most eminent occultists." Unfortunately it was found necessary to ampu-
tate one of King's eyes and he never recovered sight in the other. However
King later wrote that "while lying for several months as a patient in various hospitals" he decided he would continue writing and for the first time
would try to get his poetry published. Within a year *Mountain Idylls* was
published, and within a few more months King was married to Florence
Wheeler, to whom he had been engaged before the accident, but after his
accident he had asked her to take a year to contemplate if she still wanted
to marry a blind man. She refused to back down from her solemn vow,
they were married Christmas Day, 1901, and eventually they had two
children. At this time King was also able to sell several mining claims he
had located before his blindness and the *Ouray Herald* indicated that he
had enough money "to live life in leisure for some years to come."

Following his accident, King had somehow lost all his poetic manu-
scripts written before that time, but he rewrote many of them from memory, as well as writing many new poems. King's poems discussed personal

reflections and a search for life and death's meaning, but mostly he wrote on the beauty of the San Juans and the nature of the people that inhabited them – rugged individuals, miners, and prospectors. He also included sounds he still heard, the textures of nature he still felt, the smells he still enjoyed, and the tastes he still relished – his remaining senses were perhaps enhanced by his blindness and brings all of our senses into play when one reads or hears his poetry. He wrote of the songs of birds and the thrill of hearing a waterfall, the energy expressed by thunder or rushing water, as well as the colors (as he remembered them) and the textures of the columbine (the Colorado State Flower) and other flowers.

Alfred King's appearance fees and the sale of his two books made a respectable amount of money to augment what money he had made from selling his mining claims. And more than the money (which he didn't particularly care about) he received great praise and respect in his chosen field of endeavor. His reviews included:

> *"The soul of a poet…. The poet of the famed scenic San Juans…."* Telluride Daily Journal

> *"(He) lived among the wonderful work of nature and breathed inspiration from his surroundings…. (What he) has seen is also felt…."* The Denver Times

> *"If his verses had no other recommendation, we of the state should feel kindness toward him because of his unconcealed love and adoration of the mountains and gorges, the rock and rills, of this beautiful state."* Rocky Mountain News

Alfred Castner King died in Grand Junction, Colorado, on August 31, 1941. As Duane Smith wrote in the foreword to the reprint of King's *Mountain Idyls & Other Poems*:

> *He moved beyond localism to universal themes in a variety of subjects…. His impressions of his Colorado (mainly the San Juans) and the West are perhaps his greatest contribution. King provides a captivating, true picture of his era and the region more than many of his better known literary contemporaries. King may be largely forgotten but he left behind something very tangible.*

(This article first appeared in the *San Juan Mountain Journal*, Summer 2017)

Reverend J. J. Gibbons
One Tough Priest

≈ ≈

Several Colorado ministers, such as George Darley and John Dyer, are more famous for their missionary work, but the most amazing exploits of a "man of the cloth" in Ouray County undoubtedly belonged to a young Catholic priest J. J. Gibbons. Gibbons was assigned by the Catholic Church to lead its followers and build a church in Ouray but was to provide services throughout the San Juan Mountains. He held services in a building bought by the Catholics in Ouray that had originally been the Presbyterian Church.

Father Gibbons was born in Rhode Island but moved to Wisconsin as an infant and grew up in Iowa, where he eventually attended seminary. At first, he served in Chicago but then was sent to the Diocese of Colorado where he served for forty-five years. He was originally assigned to Georgetown, then Silver Plume, and then Leadville. When a serious epidemic broke out in the "Sky City" he worked round the clock for weeks attending to the sick and dying and holding funerals.

He was assigned to Ouray and Silverton in 1888 but lived in Ouray. He was given the responsibility for twenty mission churches in a territory that covered over 10,000 square miles of some of the most rugged territory in the Continental United States. Because of the size and ruggedness of his territory he was constantly traveling – dealing with all kinds of weather, using all kinds of transportation besides walking, and becoming involved with some extraordinary events. Father J. J. Gibbons experienced the San Juan Mountains as few men ever have. When avalanches ran, mines exploded, and plagues hit, most people backed away from the dangers, but not Father Gibbons. It was his job to tend the sick, to give last rites to the dying, bury the dead, and bring comfort to the grieving. So when life was at its grimmest, Rev. Gibbons set out, usually on foot or horseback, to bring comfort to those who needed a Catholic priest. After four years of such work he was utterly exhausted and returned to Denver where he wrote, *In the San Juan — Sketches*, which is not only a testament to his faith but also an extraordinary glimpse into life in the San Juans during its heyday of silver mining. True tales of skeletons along the high mountain trails, miners blown to bits while warming dynamite on a stove (a common practice at the time when dynamite froze), and powerful and deadly avalanches known as the "white death," are just a few of the many true tales told by the intrepid priest as related in his fascinating book.

One small example from his book was when Gibbons was in the town of Rico and a call came (telephones came early to the San Juans) to him that a miner was near death in Ouray and was asking for last rites. Gibbons had no horse until that time although he was thinking about buying one in Rico and was allowed a "test ride." He rode Bill (the animal from Rico) for eight hours and had only arrived in the small mining camp of Ophir. He had a heavy saddle, his vestments and an overcoat with him, and Bill was totally worn out.

Gibbons wrote, "It was equal to a seventy-five mile ride on the level road." From Ophir he changed horses and made Red Mountain (Town) in fifty minutes and to Ouray in forty-five more. He had crossed two ranges of mountains in the process. He found the miner sitting in a chair and "going down rapidly."

> *(The miner) raised his eyes, put out his cold hands and grasped mine, saying "Father, you came in a hurry." I said, "Yes, Fred, I was bound to be here in time, if I had to come on the saddle without a horse.... In the hush of the midnight, (the miner's) soul winged its flight to the better land. His body, with many others, lies moldering in Ouray's cemetery, awaiting the final resurrection, when there will be no more break-neck rides or death-dealing snow slides.*

DAVE DAY AND
THE SOLID MULDOON
Ouray's Eccentric Newspaper Editor

⫸ ⫷

Dave Day was a big man who fought in the Civil War and was imprisoned in both Andersonville and Florence. As a result, he had a long sabre scar down his left cheek. He was discharged after the war at the age of eighteen (he had enlisted at fourteen). In later years he gained considerable weight. He wore a big ox-bow mustache and a big brimmed cowboy-type hat. He lived in Missouri until 1881. Later his wife Victoria rode the train to Gunnison, where Dave met her and they took a stagecoach to Ouray. She remembered:

> *Mr. Day and the stagecoach driver carried guns and had revolvers slipped into their boots. She said that Day felt the Utes got a really raw deal and he opposed Otto Mears in the way he mistreated the Utes but was a close friend of his. Mears owned the toll road that Mrs. Day rode over from Gunnison on the stage and Mears later gave Day a solid gold pass for the Silverton Railroad.*

There were two newspapers in Ouray in the 1880s – one was the respectable and newsworthy *Ouray Times* and the other was Dave Day's raucous, belittling, but humorous *Solid Muldoon*. Day's paper was by far the most popular, even though the Ripley brothers' *Ouray Times* carried most of the actual news of the town and Colorado. Day and his friend Gerald Letcher brought their *Democrat* paper to Ouray from Lake City in 1879, and announced in his third issue that there was not enough business in Ouray for two papers. Day's spicy writing kept pace with the rough and tumble times of early Ouray, but some locals thought he was much too vulgar. Day claimed when he came in 1879 that Ouray "had everything including Keno and churches, bull trains and pack trains, bummers and burro punchers, sawmills and gospel mills, storms and stores, men and working women. This place impresses one as having gotten here before it was sent for." People all over Colorado waited anxiously for Day's pictur-esque and controversial weekly.

Dave Day's newspaper was even famous in some parts of Europe. Although his circulation was only 350, it included many papers outside the Town of Ouray, and the articles from his paper were often reprinted over and over in other papers across the United States. Day's writing was as caustic, offensive, and stinging as any paper of his day, and he was both hated and loved by his readers depending on what or who he was writing about. His paper gave the news exactly in the way people wanted to read it at the time. He loved "no holds barred" controversy and did not hesitate to jump into any type of fray. Although he was always fearlessly fighting for truth and justice (as he saw it), his "special way" with words made many enemies for life. Day constantly attacked other San Juan towns, such as Telluride:

Dave Day was a real character. Who else would pose while having a tur-key in his lap. The Stetson was his favorite hat.
(Courtesy of Center for Southwest Studies)

*Telluride has seven lawyers and two dance halls, 0 churches, 000 schoolhouses. Mercy what a wicked village. (*Solid Muldoon 8/17/83)

As opposed to his writing, Day was said to be very polite to visitors at his home, and he entertained often. He was said to have two pet peeves however – business women and politicians. He also roamed the bars in Ouray and later in Durango collecting news and carousing with friends. However, both Day and his wife Florence were leaders in Ouray society.

Day moved from Ouray to Durango in March 1892 and continued his paper under the name, *The Durango Democrat.* At one time or another Day was called, "controversial, opinionated, conflictive, progressive, the lover of good arguments, reformer, promoter, performer, gad-fly, and civic minded." Day liked to attack people or their ideas fearlessly and was said to carry a derringer pistol with him at all times to protect himself.

Day toured Europe in the late 1880s and was presented to Queen Victoria during this time. Day also served as a Ute Indian Agent in Ignacio at the time he was living in Durango. He died in Durango in 1914.

Day's paper made Ouray famous throughout the state. The paper's name, *Solid Muldoon* was probably a reference to a hoax – a "petrified man" that was being shown throughout the United States. Yet when asked about the name, Day replied that it came from the Zulu language and meant "virgin." His original partner said that he asked Day to come up with a name "that means something solid and honest." Day then said he came up with the idea of naming the paper after William Muldoon, one of the greatest promoters of prize fights at the time in New York City. Another possibility was that there was a popular song at the time that included the words "As I walk the street each friend I meet says 'There goes Muldoon – He is a solid man.'"

Day often wrote or printed bawdy poetry in the paper. One example:

> *Here lie the bones of poor old Charlotte,*
> *Born a virgin but died a harlot;*
> *For eighteen years she preserved her virginity,*
> *A damn good record for this vicinity.*

Another example was when he printed an article about a masquerade ball in Silverton and wrote: "The ladies of Silverton never look quite so beautiful as when they are at a masquerade ball."

Day's wit and sarcasm, coupled with his recklessness about the truth, may never be equaled in the history of journalism. He bragged that he had no religion, had forty-two libel suits pending against him at one time, that he had never paid a dime in judgment (he did not say if he actually won all the cases), and that for ten days he had been locked in jail for criticizing a judge. However he only got shot at on one occasion.

Day's wife Victoria Folck, who he met in Missouri, was proud that her husband wrote of the unfair treatment the Utes received after the Meeker Massacre. Day also wrote badly of Otto Mears and the way he treated the Utes in 1880, even though Mears was considered a friend. Mrs. Day said she worried a lot about his being shot at by men he had written bad things about.

CHARLES HALL
The Forty-Eight Pound Man

Of all the survival stories of frantic men lost in the San Juan Mountain wilderness, the story of Charles L. Hall certainly ranks as the most incredible – perhaps even the most amazing in all the Rocky Mountains. Charles was raised in New York State and Iowa and studied law and ministry in college. After hearing about the Pike's Peak Gold Rush, he came to Colorado, and initially started a cattle ranch, then sold out in December 1859 to prospect in California Gulch near today's Leadville. He was only moderately successful there, so he joined with two partners (named Dick Harris or Harrison and Miles O'Neal) and headed for the San Juan Mountains. The men were supposedly part of the "Turner Group" but soon split off on their own. They entered the San Juans from the south, and discovered that there were men from several other groups scattered all over the mountains looking unsuccessfully for gold to pan.

The men went all the way up the upper Animas Forks River to reach the headwaters of the Uncompahgre River, passed downriver through the site of the future Ouray, panned for gold in Cow Creek, and eventually ended up back in Baker's Park. It was evidently a little too crowded for them there and the larger group had no extra supplies. Hall later related that both Kit Carson and Albert Pfeiffer had suggested (presumably back in New Mexico) that they come out of the San Juans by way of the lower Animas and Los Piños Rivers and winter in Abiqui or Taos, but they headed back to the site of the future Ouray. By this time it was the dead of winter and the three men were running desperately short on food. They boiled their flour sacks to make a very light broth. They ate their buckskin clothes, boiled their boots, and finally even boiled the buffalo robe they had been using for warmth when sleeping in the winter weather.

Hall remembered a camp on the Uncompahgre near the Ouray bowl where a man named Nate Hurd had left some hides. Somehow they made it back there through the deep snow and ice and boiled those hides for what nutrition they could get out of them. Soon after this time Hall began to realize that his two companions were plotting to kill and eat him. He finally got away from his companions but was totally lost and discovered they were following him through the deep snow. All three were extremely weak and had to travel by crawling on the hands and knees, traveling about a mile a day. Hall would fire his pistol periodically, hoping someone would hear it besides his two ex-partners and respond. One day his shot was heard near Engineer Mountain by men that were in the Henson Creek drainage but who came around the mountain to respond.

Charles Hall

Hall was saved by a future Governor of Colorado, Benjamin H. Eaton and others. By this time Hall weighed only forty-eight pounds, and it was said that his jacket was frozen to his body and could not be easily removed. However he totally recovered and went back to California Gulch for more prospecting. He discovered a salt spring between there and Fairplay and began boiling and selling salt. Later he went into politics, and eventually was a very successful prospector and politician in Colorado and Arizona.

THE RIPLEY BROTHERS
Believe It or Not

⁓ ⁓

In 1877 Henry Ripley and his brother William came from Cañon City, where they had operated *The Cañon City Times* for five years, to Ouray over Otto Mears' just finished toll road from Saguache to Lake City, and the new Los Piños Agency and Ouray. The Ripley brothers had decided to join "The San Juan Excitement" and opened the first newspaper in the Uncompahgre Valley. Their month long journey to the booming mining town was a rough one. Henry even reported that the only evidence of a road was being "held up periodically for a toll." The Ripleys were part of the large number of really good men who were in the San Juans at this time; although it seems that we tend to remember the bad or off beat personalities, there were many more "good men." Henry Ripley was awarded the prestigious medal of Honor for his actions at Vicksburg. After Dave Day opened the *Solid Muldoon* several years later, they were usually referred to as Ouray's "other newspaper," but they persevered. As opposed to *The Solid Muldoon*, *The Times* was a Republican paper.

The Ripleys stayed for a decade during much of which Day was famous all over Colorado, but eventually (after the Ripleys had left) Day was forced to leave town. As opposed to Day, the Ripleys reported the news in a careful and dignified way; but, of course, it is Day that history remembers and not the Ripley brothers. Yet it was their fair and level-headed reporting that helped make Ouray what it is today. It was a way of doing business that today's newspaper men should remember.

Ripley wrote in his book, *The Handclasp of the East and West*:

> *…If there should come a regret, it will be that we did not enter more heartily into the great work, had been less self-seeking and more thoughtful of the welfare of those coming after; had realized that every stone removed from the highway, every tree that was*

planted for the beautifying of our streets, was not merely for "me and mine," but for the good of all, to exemplify the prophecy, "the desert shall blossom as the rose."

Ripley's dedication to his book *Handclasp of the East and West* shows his love for the other Ouray pioneers:

To the brave men who dared
The loving women who endured,
The children who drank in the greatness of
This western life and helped make it what we see today;
To the east who gave to these people the rich
Legacy of the forefathers, the undaunted
Spirit of overcoming, the spirit of doing, this book is dedicated

The first issue of their paper appeared on June 16, 1877. Ripley wrote later in his book:

A great day it was for Ouray when the first paper was printed. All day long men came to the office to see how things were progressing.

Henry Ripley, editor of the Ouray Times *is at the center of this photo. The* Ouray Times' *office is second from the left. The building at the right in the far rear is the infamous 220 saloon.*   (Author's Collection)

The first copy, as was usual in such cases, was put up at auction and sold for ten dollars… The paper was made as much of as the advent of the first baby, and well it might, for its travail in getting there had been long and hard.

The Ripleys worked mainly in the office, setting type and doing printing work for the people of the town. They relied on a reporter or two to bring them the latest news. The price for their paper was two dollars a year, and they took anything in payment – money, gold dust, vegetables from the local gardens, firewood, and future promises to pay.

After the Ute Indians were removed from the Uncompahgre Valley, the Ripleys decided in 1886 to move to near Montrose and become farmers and ranchers. They even got involved with mining. Dave Day and his *Solid Muldoon* may have been known better but the Ripleys left more of a legacy. The Ripleys sold their paper when they left Ouray and it became the *Ouray Budget* and then the *Ouray Plaindealer*, which still exists today. Henry Ripley called his book *The Handclasp of the East and West* as he very firmly believed that the West could never have been conquered without the help, and especially with capital, from the people of the East. However Ripley autobiography uses "pen names" for himself and some others in his book, which was a common practice of the time, but sometimes makes it hard for today's historians to decide who did what.

THE NOTORIOUS MARLOW BROTHERS
Outlaws Turned Sheriff Deputies

The five Marlow brothers and their mother and father started earning their notoriety in the panhandle of Indian Territory (now Oklahoma), where they were suspected of taking stray cattle from the huge cattle drives that were passing through Oklahoma from Texas to the railroad in Kansas at that time. This action was not illegal, but some people suggested that the cattle taken were not strays, but cut out of the large herds by the Marlows. William Marlow died in 1865 leaving Martha Marlow with his four children by a previous marriage and two by her. However Martha was a very strong woman – a descendant of Daniel Boone. Then one day a posse came to the Marlow house to arrest Boone Marlow for shooting a drunken cowboy who had pulled a gun on him. Boone swore the shooting was in self-defense. The posse also claimed Boone was wanted for stealing horses, but the complainant had already notified the deputy that he had found his horses. Nevertheless the deputy entered the Marlow home and shot at Boone while the family was eating dinner. When Boone shot back he hit the local Sheriff. While the Marlow family was trying to help the Sheriff, Boone escaped and when brother Epp was sent to get the doctor for the Sheriff, he was arrested. Then a posse arrested George, Charles, and Alf Boone, even though they were not at home at the time of the shooting. The brothers were sent to Graham, Texas, where the cowboy had been shot. Graham had a bad reputation for mob violence, and the brothers tried to escape, but were quickly recaptured. When a mob did come for them the next night, the Marlow brothers fought them off. The Graham sheriffs' office was then ordered to move the brothers to Ft. Worth.

The four brothers were chained two by two to each other (Boone was still at large) and taken to wagons for transport. The brothers quickly noted that many of the men transporting them were part of the mob that had attacked them the night before. About a mile out of Graham the wagons stopped and a mob attacked. A battle ensued in which three of the posse (which had all been a part of the mob) were killed and three were badly wounded. Epp and Alfred Marlow were killed. George and Charles were wounded and had to cut the feet off their dead brothers to get out of the chains. Charles had been shot through one of his lungs. Members of the mob were later arrested, charged with murder, and found guilty. George and Charles were arrested, tried, and found not guilty of the killing of the Sheriff and of the underlying charge of being horse thieves. They then moved to Colorado and eventually to Ouray County.

Two of the top Texas Rangers of the time came to Ouray County in 1890 to try to arrest and take the Marlow brothers back to Texas, but the locals protected the Marlows by warning them that law officers from out of the area were on the train and helping to hide them while the officers were there. A mob even surrounded the out-of-state officers and told them they would not let them take the Marlows. The governors of both

Charles Marlow (left) and George Marlow (right) posed wearing their guns, carrying their rifles and proudly displaying their Deputy Sheriff badges.

(Courtesy of Wikipedia)

Texas and Colorado became involved in the event, and it was determined the Texas Rangers had no jurisdiction over the case.

George and Charley became Ouray County Deputy Sheriffs and were deputized on several occasions by other Colorado county sheriffs when help was needed in their counties. The most famous action of the two brother's was joining Sheriff Doc Shores and a few other deputies to help quell a large, armed labor strike in Crested Butte.

Eventually Ouray County Judge William Rathmell acted as a ghost writer for the Marlow's book, *The Life of the Marlows*. In the 1950s a screenwriter read the book, bought the rights, and the story was told in the movie *The Sons of Katie Elder*, with the roles of the two Marlows, who eventually lived many years in Ouray, played by Dean Martin and John Wayne. There have also been several books written on the entire family.

The Marlow brothers and their mother are buried on their eventual homestead on Billy Creek near the little town of Colona.

EVALYN WALSH MCCLEAN
And The Purchase of the Hope Diamond

❧   ❧

It is often written or told incorrectly that after Tom Walsh struck it rich in Imogene Basin at what became the upper Camp Bird Mine that he then bought his only daughter, Evalyn, the Hope Diamond. Walsh did enjoy his riches and used them lavishly, especially on his daughter Evalyn, but he did not buy her the diamond except in a very indirect way. Several years after their rich discovery (1897) the Walshs moved from Ouray to Washington, D. C. Two years later President McKinley appointed Tom Walsh a Commissioner to the Paris Exposition, and Evalyn went with the family to France. To say she was spoiled by that time puts it mildly. At age twelve she slipped liquor out of her father's liquor closet, squandered her allowance on whims like dozens of ermine tails, and caused several governesses to quit their jobs. She also had her own carriage and coachman to take her to and from school.

In 1905 Evelyn's brother was killed in an auto accident that also injured Evelyn and left her with one leg shorter than the other. At age fourteen Evelyn was sent back to France to live and take singing lessons. There she enjoyed a wild life that included coloring her hair (a very wild act at the time) and drinking lots of alcohol. She married Edward Beale McLean in July 1908. McLean was the son of the *Washington Post* newspaper owner John R. McClean. The newlyweds were both only twenty-two years old and their fathers gave each of them $100,000 to spend on their proposed six month honeymoon in Africa and Europe. In less than four months they had run out of the $200,000 allocated for their honeymoon (millions in today's dollars). Walsh sent his daughter more money. McClean's father told him to come home. Just before leaving Europe, Evelyn realized that she still had not bought the special "wedding present" that her father had asked her to buy herself. She of course wanted the best available and went to Cartier's in Paris to look for jewelry. The necklace she chose cost $120,000 and not only contained the 95 carat Star of the East Diamond but also contained a 34 ½ carat emerald and a 32 ½ grain pearl. However none were the Hope Diamond. Cartier's gave the couple credit to buy the necklace, which Evalyn hoped she could talk her father into buying for her as a combination wedding and Christmas present. Evalyn did not first see the Hope diamond until several years later, when she saw a member of a Sultan's family wearing it and supposedly said she had to have it (Evalyn denied this later in her book).

Later, in 1910, Cartier brought the Hope Diamond to Evalyn. It was six months after the birth of her first child and only a few months after the death of her father. Cartier told her the diamond was supposed to bring bad luck to anyone who owned it, and Evalyn passed on a purchase at that time. However Cartier tried again some months later. This time she said she would think about buying the diamond and Cartier shrewdly let her keep the diamond for a while. She ended up trading in many pieces of her jewelry on the purchase, including some of the jewelry her father had bought her, and even then she had to pay the balance in installments. Soon, after buying the necklace, she took it to a priest to be blessed. She would often wear the Hope necklace with the Star of the East and a third necklace of large diamonds – all at the

Evalyn Walsh McClean posed with the blue Hope Diamond, the Star of the East and a gold chain set with emeralds.
(Author's Collection)

same time. It was said that she also let her Great Dane wear the Hope Diamond on occasion.

Evalyn had four children including Vinson McClean who was killed by a car at age nine, and a daughter Evalyn that died of a pill overdose at age twenty-five. She herself died on April 26, 1947. Evalyn had by then lost most of her fortune. The Hope Diamond was sold to jeweler Harry Winston for $176,920 to help pay her debts. It is now in the Smithsonian Museum. The Star of the East brought $185,000. Was the curse of the Hope diamond at work?

Evalyn Walsh McClean once said that "one can never wear enough jewelry." She was pushing that limit here.

(Author's Collection)

LOUIS KING
Ouray's #1 Promoter And His Tiny Stagecoach

Although not a mine owner, Louis King was a very respected member of Ouray society from its earliest days. He was born in 1842 in Germany and came to Ouray in 1877. He was a blacksmith and stable owner, but mainly a wheel maker and was in great demand as the rough San Juan country took a huge toll on wagon wheels. Louis was very well-liked and a powerhouse in Ouray political circles. He came to Ouray at the age of thirty-five after the death of his wife in 1876. His daughter Elizabeth was Ouray's first school teacher – teaching forty-six students in 1876-77. In 1878 King was elected the President of Ouray's first Board of Trade, and he became very prominent through his many efforts to promote Ouray. He became a county commissioner for Ouray County in 1893 and in 1899 was appointed a Commissioner of the State of Colorado Penitentiary. King was fairly well off when the Silver Panic hit Colorado but lost most of his wealth at that time, as he had invested heavily or taken trade for part ownership in many of the local mines.

One of King's best ideas was building a one-half scale stage that was pulled by Shetland ponies and which he took to parades or conventions in other towns. The stage was probably built at his business next to City Hall. Everything worked on his miniature stage just as on a real stage, except everything was smaller. The stagecoach was built in late 1890s for the use of Ouray Elks Lodge but also for King's grandchildren to play with. King would often drive the stage himself pulled by two Shetland ponies, which made it look like a giant was sitting on it. The stagecoach was a great hit and in great demand.

Another way of promoting Ouray that King came up with was a band with musicians that dressed as cowboys, complete with wooly chaps, cowboy hats, scarfs around their necks, cowboy boots, etc. The band originated in Kansas City but eventually made its way to Silverton where it became the Silverton Cowboy Band and then moved to Ouray where it was the Ouray Cowboy Band. After Ouray the band moved to Creede.

In Ouray the band started using King's little stagecoach by carrying the band's large drum strapped in the luggage "boot" at the back of the stage. The band would also carry banners promoting Ouray and its businesses. Once again it was a great hit and the band was always in great demand.

King's original business location was below the Main Street level and behind the Story Block. After fire destroyed his two story frame building at the corner of Seventh and Main, King built what is now called the Story Block. Other businesses leased the upper two stories, But King lost the building at foreclosure to William Story. The spot was King's livery stable before the brick building's construction, which was completed in 1892. King's previous operation was then moved to where Ouray's community building is now located. King died in 1904 and the band bought and still used King's little stagecoach to carry its huge drum.

Louis King's ½ scale stage made a great hit with the local kids. It is seen here in front of Ouray's original City Hall before it burned. Kings shop would be just to the right of the photo.

(Author's Collection)

CHIPETA
Queen of the Utes

⚊⚊

Chipeta, Chief Ouray's lovely, spirited, and loyal wife, was described by one writer as "a personality plus princess," and as a young woman she captivated everyone who met her – Ute or White. The title "Queen of the Utes" was originally used in a derogatory manner by an American journalist, but as the Whites came to know her it came to be used as a compliment. She sang beautifully in Ute or Spanish, played the guitar, danced, and was generally the life of the party. She also was a very good hunter and a deadly shot with her Winchester rifle. She spoke fairly good English, Ute, and some Spanish. Perhaps most importantly she was Chief Ouray's main adviser and confidant – and good at it. She recognized the American's great superiority in warfare and always counseled for peace with the Whites and was friendly (although wary) with them. This created a very fine line between being thought of as a traitor by other Utes and keeping her people from being annulated. There were several times when Ouray was so disgusted with the Americans not keeping their promises to the Utes that he was leaning towards going to war, because not keeping one's solemn word was unthinkable to a Ute. But Chipeta calmed him down and made him choose peace over war. On occasion she was even invited into councils with the Utes chiefs to express her opinion – almost unheard of for a Native American woman.

After Chief Ouray's death some sources wrote that Chipeta was almost made the overall chief of the Ute tribe, as she was the only person that the Utes could all agree upon. She was one of the Ute leaders before Ouray's death, and she often sat in on councils of the various subchiefs; however taking Ouray's spot as overall chief of the Utes would have been highly unlikely, as only men held the position of a chief. After Chief Ouray's death she chose to leave Colorado with her Tabeguache band, giving up the nice homestead that the U. S. built for her and

Ouray and which they had lived in for about five years. The Americans not only told her that she could stay but even tried to convince her to do so. Perhaps she was totally disgusted with the American actions and failure to keep their promises, but she never indicated any bitterness to the Whites. The fact that she did not stay in Colorado shows that she was determined to give up all of the American way of life and live with her people. There is even a legend that Chipeta threw a bag of U. S. gold coins that she and Ouray had saved into the Black Canyon in disgust. Such an action was possible as there are clues that she was very saddened and felt strongly that her people had been betrayed.

Late in her life Chipeta again associated with the Whites and became a celebrity – appearing in parades, being invited into people's homes, and usually drawing a crowd of Whites wherever she appeared. She especially liked to be around the Americans that she and Ouray had been with in her younger years. Chipeta loved children (she had none of her own), but she took in dozens of unwanted

Chipeta was a Kiowa Apache, found alone at a young age by Utes. Yet she captured the hearts of many Utes and Whites. She probably made the outfit she wears in this photo.

(Author's Collection)

or orphan Ute children over the years, most of whom consider her their mother or grandmother. Chipeta died at about age eighty, almost forty-five years after Ouray died. She was originally buried in a shallow grave near her tepee in Utah, but when it was heard that animals were disturbing her grave, Montrose residents got permission to have her reinterred there at the present site of the Ute Museum.

MARIE SCOTT
The Lady Always Wore Blue Jeans

❧ ❧

Women ranchers were few and far between in the Old West, but Ouray County had a bigger than life exception – Marie Scott. Marie was not the first lady rancher in Colorado, but she was probably the most successful, to the point that she has become a legend. Her Alpine Meadows Ranch, which was headquarters in Ridgway, eventually included large chunks of land that spread all the way from Ridgway to the Utah border. Marie didn't look the part of a lady rancher. She was very petite (five feet tall with red hair and blue eyes). However it was said that she could outride, out rope and shoot a gun better than any Colorado cowboy, a fact that was never tested but which was probably true.

Most of the successful women ranchers in Colorado did not start their own ranches. Almost all of them inherited their ranches from their fathers or husbands, but since a woman rancher

Marie Scott loved dogs and cats (Blaze is shown with her). She also loved to spend time on hunting or line cabins that she owned far up in the mountains. This one was called "The Back of the Moon.)
(Author's Collection)

did much of the work on their ranch, they were able to continue and do well with them. Marie's mother was a school teacher, who married Bartley Scott, a small but self-sufficient Ridgway rancher who unfortunately died young at age thirty-four. Her mother had very little knowledge of ranching but did the best she could. Marie's grandfather filled in somewhat as a father, but it was Marie's mother that mostly influenced her life. Marie's mother ran the ranch as best as she could, but Marie really wanted to be a rancher – the best and most successful rancher she could be. Fortunately Marie's Mom turned the ranch over to her while Marie was still a teenager. Before Marie was even twenty, she had also bought a place of her own. Although she eventually inherited her father's ranch, it was only a very small part of what she accomplished. She died a wealthy, legendary woman who owned more land than perhaps any other woman on the Western Slope of Colorado. Much of her ranch is now owned by fashion designer Ralph Lauren.

Marie took over her father's ranch shortly before a very bad economic time for most ranchers – the Great Depression – but Marie saw it as a time of opportunity. She also had a little luck. She sold part of her herd of cattle shortly before the depression hit, and she used to money to buy other ranches, many with their own cattle that she would sell and buy another ranch. She also lived very simply in a small house, and even when she was quite rich she did the same. Her ranch and her house were really not distinguishable from her neighbors. She used a wood and coal burning stove for heat and cooking. She was said to buy just one pair of blue jeans at a time, which she wore all the time until they totally wore out. Then she would buy one more pair. In September of 1929 she married Bob Valiant, who had his own little herd. Marie was now thirty and some say she fell for Bob's Herford herd and not for Bob Valiant. Both of them were very strong-willed and the marriage did not last long. After the divorce Marie bought Bob's ranch and made him her overall foreman! She often said he made a much better foreman than he did a husband.

Eventually Marie Scott owned an immense amount of land. She was constantly buying, selling, and trading and no one is sure just how much land she owned, but a good guess would be between 60,000 and 100,000 acres. Even though she owned so much land she kept her now purebred Herford herd small, usually about 300 head that she kept near her home. Neighbors and friends often leased her land for their cattle and sheep. However she always fenced her land if it wasn't fenced when she bought it. It was said that at one time her range riders were keeping up 300 miles of fence!

In her old age Marie did begin to sell some of her land, some of which had cabins on them. At the time of her death she was down to about 25,000 acres, most of it near her home. Marie had no heirs and she gave most of her land and money to friends and employees before she died. Marie Scott died November 5, 1979 and what land and money was left after expenses and taxes went to friends and relatives.

In Ouray, as opposed to many mining camps, there were many educated and refined women. This photo shows the women at the Guston Mine about 1890. Unfortunately not many of their actions were recorded.
(Author's Photo)

Places

DID CHIEF OURAY HAVE
A HOUSE IN OURAY?
He Did Like the Hot Springs

❧ ❧

The U. S. government built a nice adobe house for Chief Ouray near today's Montrose about 1875. Ouray, Chipeta and several of their employees lived there for about five years until Chief Ouray's death and the removal of the Utes from Colorado. However it has also been written that Chief Ouray had an adobe house in Ouray on the hillside behind today's Wiesbaden spa. That there was an adobe house at that spot is certain. Although nothing remains of the house today, William Henry Jackson took photos of it in the late 1880s. This author first saw one of the photos in the 1980s in a William Henry Jackson collection of the Colorado Historical Society. The house was definitely old and crumbling at the time that photo was taken (indicating it may have been built before there was a town of Ouray when the site was Ute land), but the heavy snows in Ouray could quickly destroy an adobe building that wasn't being kept up. The photo was labeled only "Ouray's House," but the label could have been created long after Jackson's time, perhaps at the time the photograph was obtained by the Colorado Historical Society.

The author brought the photo to the attention of archeologist/anthropologist Steve Baker, who eventually excavated parts of the house's foundation and verified that an old adobe house once stood there, but nothing was found at that time that would directly connect it to Chief Ouray or a Ute. It was of New Mexico style, probably similar to the one Ouray lived in as a child when indentured to a Spanish couple, and as shown in the accompanying photo, the home was only one room and contained a New Mexico style fireplace in one corner. The house was next to a hot water spring that is no longer there since the Wiesbaden expanded its hot water operation. The house would have had a commanding view of the Ouray bowl, and Chief Ouray did like to soak in hot spring pools for his arthritis.

There are two photos of "Ouray's house in Ouray" taken by William Henry Jackson in the late 1880s – this one, and one taken from a distance. It was evidently built from adobe before Whites came to Ouray.

(Author's Collection)

Several people in Ouray opposed the statement that this was Chief Ouray's house. The building was definitely not typical of the Town of Ouray, which in the early days had plenty of trees before they were cut down for log cabins, but little or none of the clay needed for an adobe building. Most of all, there is no indication in the history books or the local newspapers that Chief Ouray ever had a home in the future City of Ouray, but he was built an adobe home in near the future City of Montrose. He had two homes built of log at the first Los Piños Agency on Cochetopa Pass (one burned down and was replaced by another.) The Utes did not typically live in adobe structures, preferring the teepee and wickiups since they were very mobile.

It has been argued by some of those that feel Chief Ouray had a house in the City of Ouray that the photograph carries William Henry Jackson's identification that it is Ouray's home and that Jackson was very careful to document the history of the places shown in his photographs. On the other hand no one knows who put the label on the photograph. However one wonders why Jackson took the photo in the first place if it did not have some kind of significance.

THE WESTERN HOTEL
"The Miner's Palace" and a Secret Tunnel

The Western Hotel was built in Ouray by Frances Carney in 1892 at the corner of Seventh Avenue and Second Street. The western side of the hotel was directly across Second Street from Ouray's substantial red light district. Seventh Avenue (where the front of the hotel is located) was the access to and from the railroad depot from Main (Third) Street, and as such the spot was a good location for a hotel (although not on Main Street). However respectable businesses (and the hotel itself was respectable) generally stayed south of Seventh Avenue and west of Second Street. The Western Hotel was therefore located in kind of a "no-man's land" between the two areas. Bordellos on this section of Second Street included The Bird Cage, The Clipper, The Bon Ton (not the restaurant), the Monte Carlo, Morning Star, and the Temple of Music. The Gold Belt Dance Hall and Roma Saloon complex (the largest in Ouray) was only a block further northeast. At one time there were almost 100 women "on the line" in Ouray, many of them on Second Street. There were also thirty-five saloons and quite a few dance halls in the town. Of course the more respectable hotel residents did not wish to be seen going to those areas, but they were reported by some to use a tunnel or a below the ground exit out the back (north side) of the Western Hotel basement to avoid detection.

The wooden hotel (the largest wooden structure in Ouray and originally called "The Monte Alta") was not for the upper class, (it is now a wonderfully authentic experience of a typical 1900s hotel) but it was very nicely built and furnished. The three-story hotel had a very large dining room for its guests and had forty-three sleeping rooms, three toilets, but only one bathtub. There was an opening through the roof of the hotel on the inside second and third floors that allowed sunlight for the interior rooms. The owners billed the hotel as "The Miner's Palace." Room and board was $1.25 a day in 1896 or six dollars a week. It also had a saloon with doors near the hotel's check-in counter and also doors to the street, and next to that was a small gambling room. The hotel became a boarding house in 1916, and has been refurbished several times in the last few decades.

The Western Motel was showing its age in 1942. If you look carefully you can see some of the tourists on the front porch.
(Author's Collection)

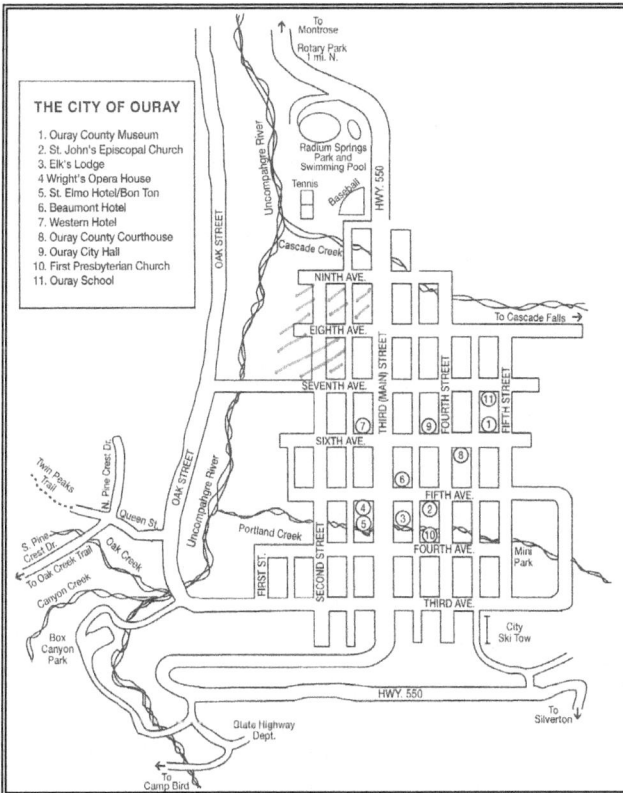

THE CITY OF OURAY

1. Ouray County Museum
2. St. John's Episcopal Church
3. Elk's Lodge
4 Wright's Opera House
5. St. Elmo Hotel/Bon Ton
6. Beaumont Hotel
7. Western Hotel
8. Ouray County Courthouse
9. Ouray City Hall
10. First Presbyterian Church
11. Ouray School

The Hashed area was the heart of the Red Light area.
(Map property of Author)

THE ST. ELMO HOTEL
And Aunt Kittie

⁓ ⁓

Kitty Heit was an enterprising young woman who came to Ouray about 1886 and bought an inexpensive restaurant (the Bon Ton) next to Ouray's Wright's Opera House. Kitty managed it for a while, and it was frequented by miners and others who wanted a good meal for their money. The local paper said that the Bon Ton "combines excellent cuisine and courteous treatment to a degree that renders (eating there) rather home-like. It is by far the best establishment of its kind in Ouray." Kitty did have good business sense and a kind heart. Her place soon became very popular and successful; in fact, it was so successful that she was able to open a substantial brick hotel (the St. Elmo) next to the restaurant in 1898. Everyone loved "Aunt Kitty (sometimes spelled "Kittie," she was the premier business woman in Ouray. When she died of a heart attack in May 1915 the *Ouray Herald* wrote:

> *Her many acts of kindness and charity are legion and she was recognized as the miner's friend. They were always welcome at her home whether flush with money or down and out. Her hotel came about as a real home for the lonesome and homeless and everything was done for "her boys. During her residence in Ouray she had become a regular "mother" to hundreds and no one could possibly be missed more than she.*

Aunt Kitty's restaurant adjoined the Wright Opera House (completed in 1888) on the south side (where the patio is now) and she catered to theatre goers, both before and after performances. The Bon Ton was also popular with Circle Route passengers as the stage portion of the route to Silverton started at the Bon Ton or the Beaumont. The south end of Ouray's Main Street became the place for the "nicer people" in town in the late 1880s and early 1900s since it contained Mrs. Heit's two establishments, the Elks Club, the Wright's Opera

Aunt Kitty and friends stand in front of her two establishments a little before the turn of the century.   (Author's Collection)

House, the Beaumont Hotel, Arps large hardware store, several other nice hotels, and many other boarding and business establishments visited by the gentlemen and women visitors to the town. The rougher establishments, including the red light district and many of the bars, were generally at the north end of town.

Typical room and board rates in the 1880s were $1.25 a day or six to eight dollars a week. Meals alone were twenty-five to fifty cents. Room and board was about three times higher at the Beaumont. Kitty's restaurant was torn down in 1924 but the Bon Ton Italian restaurant now operates in the basement of her St. Elmo Hotel and has expanded slightly into the area Kittie's restaurant used to occupy. The St. Elmo Hotel had been refurbished with 1900s attire and the Bon Ton restaurant has been serving some of the best food on the Western Slope of Colorado for three decades.

THE BEAUMONT HOTEL
Kings Stayed Here

The Beaumont Hotel was built by a local group of men (The Ouray Real Estate and Building Association) with the intention of being Ouray's premier building, both in appearance and in location. It was meant to impress capitalists from the East and Europe that often visited Ouray to look at the area's mines and to give a sense of permanence to the city as opposed to a "mining camp." Its construction started in July 1886, the building cost $85,000, and it officially opened in June 1887 and had its grand opening ball in July 1887. Col. Charles Nix loaned the group part of the money to build the hotel but foreclosed and became owner in February 1893. People from all over the San Juans attended the grand opening and the hotel soon had the nickname of "The Flagship of the San Juans." The hotel was one of Ouray's first buildings to use electricity and a street light hung at the middle of the intersection outside the hotel, which was very unusual for a time when many eastern cities didn't have street lights. The hotel was heated by steam and had forty-six sleeping rooms. Some of these rooms were small and some were very luxurious and spacious.

The Miner's and Merchant's Bank was located in the southeast corner, the Bank of Ouray was in the middle of the hotel and a merchandise business was on the north end of the ground floor. Other fine businesses were located in these spots over the years. A three-story center atrium allowed sunlight to reach all three floors, and a large staircase still travels half way to the second floor and then splits into two sweeping accesses for the second floor. The stairway for the third floor is near the back of the building. Fine Navajo blankets were displayed on the balconies of the second and third floors looking down into the lobby. The southern corner of the ground floor also featured a billiards room for its guest's entertainment and a barber shop. Its dining room was on the second floor, was two stories tall, and featured a

The Beaumont was and is one of the premier hotels in Colorado. The Circle Route Stage (See page 90) stands in front of the hotel and Ouray's electric street light hangs in the upper left corner.   (Author's Collection)

small orchestra pit overlooking the dining guests and rosewood paneling. Both the food and the setting in the dining room were first-class. Sarah Berhart and Lillie Langtree stayed and performed at the hotel. The hotel was one of several large brick buildings built in Ouray in the 1880s and it did give the town a definite sense of permanence, as opposed to many other Colorado mining towns.

Not only was the building beautiful, but it was also lavishly furnished throughout and decorated with gold velour wallpaper and redwood paneling. Its furniture came from Marshall Field's in Chicago (as the original manager of the hotel also owned an interest in that business). It featured William Henry Jackson photos of the area and glass display cases showing fine specimens of gold, silver, and other minerals from the local mines. Charles Nix, who originally rented and later owned the hotel, was a hotel magnate from Chicago, who brought some of his staff to Ouray to train the locals for their jobs at the hotel. He also brought a beautiful black carriage with four matching horses that was used to bring guests to and from the railroad station to the Beaumont.

There are many myths concerning visitors who supposedly stayed at the Beaumont or their antics while there. Herbert Hoover did actually sleep in the hotel, but it was while he was a young mining engineer and before he became president. King Leopold from Belgium was said to have belayed himself down the interior atrium of the hotel. The hotel had two entrances – one on Main Street and the other on the south side of the building on Fifth Avenue for ladies, who were not supposed to use the front entrance, as no respectable woman at the time would supposedly enter a hotel from the town's Main Street. However the entrance also allowed some "risqué" women to get into the hotel without being seen. The hotel declined after the Silver Crash of 1893, but still was a very nice hotel. Most of Ouray's major social events were held at the Beaumont dining and ball room until the Great Depression days. After WWII it was refurnished and improved again, but the owners couldn't compete with the new movement toward staying in motels, and hotels fell out of favor. The last regular owners in the twentieth century closed the hotel in 1964 and sold it to Wayland Phillips of west Chicago and Ridgway in April 1967. Phillips kept the hotel closed, moved most of the furnishings out, and let the hotel decay for thirty-five years, supposedly because she was upset at some of the residents of Ouray.

Dan King and his wife Mary spent $6 million restoring the hotel to its original grandeur. It is said they paid $850,000 for the hotel itself. The Kings did such a marvelous job of restoration that it earned them several major preservation and restoration awards. King sold the Beaumont to the Leavers who maintain their high standards.

Miners in this Harper's Weekly *sketch (9/19/1894) are in a hot mineral cave after having an accident or to help cure respiratory problem, arthritis, or rheumatism.* (Author's Collection)

OURAY COUNTY'S RADIOACTIVE SOAKING POOLS
But They Cured People

〜 〜

At the beginning of the twentieth century, radium was being touted as a medical cure for many illnesses and maladies. There were radium clinics and various radium machines in use all over the United States and Europe. Ouray at one time featured the "natural" radium of its hot springs. This was before the present-day swimming pool was built, and Ouray advertised that it had several radioactive pools and caves and even that those pools had the "most radioactive water in the world," which was not a true statement. The water was and is perfectly safe. It was also advertised throughout the United States that the Ouray pools could cure almost any ailment. Most of the reported cures were of rheumatism and breathing problems.

The Sweet Skin in Ouray advertised its radioactive hot springs' water as a cure-all. Evidently the elk thought it might also be good for what ailed them.
(Author's Collection)

Two of the early commercial hot springs baths/pools or places to drink the hot water were the Cogar Hot Springs Bath and the Sweetskin near the far south end of town. The western and southern side of Ouray's hillsides seemed to be covered with small springs (as well as the large spring on the eastern slope at Buchanon's bath house), and several of the smaller springs were eventually incorporated into residential use for heating, fish ponds, decorative pools of lilies, and even for heat in the winter. One early Ouray resident said there were over 100 spots where hot water seeped from the ground within Ouray's city limits. William Weston, a local mine owner, had one such small pool for his gold fish, but a later owner drained the pool, sent the fish to the present pool site, and built a house on the spot. The Buchanon bathhouse, was the predecessor of the Wiesbaden at the east side of town. "Mother Buchanon's" bath house and caves were used extensively by miners who came to town to recover from injuries, rheumatism, or lung related diseases caused by the high altitude and wet conditions in which they worked. It was written that "the spring was hot enough that it was tempered with cold water." Rev. Gibbons wrote that there was not a finer woman in town than Mother Buchanon and that her head "brimmed with sympathy and good humor, and well she deserved her title of endearment." Her husband was called "the General" but was also well-liked and was also known to be very generous.

In the 1920s Buchanon's was called "The Radium Vapor Health Institute" and run by Dr. C. V. Bates, who also ran the hospital across the street and proposed an underground tunnel from the hospital, under the Catholic Church to the spring. It is unknown if the tunnel was completed. If it was it may be another "Secret" tunnel in Ouray. Among other things he advertised "Electric Treatments" as a cure. Parts of this spring may have been used in connection with the "Chief Ouray" house described elsewhere in this book.

Bates also advertised that his spring contained the highest percentage of radioactivity of any in the world and claimed cures from kidney diseases, but he also noted that "all of the surroundings at Ouray conduce to the restoration of health to the afflicted." Another physician reported that the radioactive waters "offer the most abundant opportunity for the establishment of a child's clinic for neglected and undernourished children of the East...."

The Buchanon's four baths (a door for each) are at left and their house at right. In the back behind the house is "Chief Ouray's" house.
(Author's Collection)

A.G. "Doc" Dunbarton's 's two story bath house, was built in 1890 almost in the middle of downtown Ouray and was indoors. His place, called simply Dunbarton's Pool," was filled with the overflow hot water coming from the Buchanon bath house, which was piped down the street. It was probably the largest private hot springs pool in town during its time, and featured six hot baths (which could be rented for twenty-five cents). Later it was owned by the Mcleods who decorated the pool area with their sea shell collection and rented rooms to miners on the second floor. The building was eventually destroyed by fire and the pool filled in.

Major hot springs were also known in Box Canyon and were used by several nearby establishments, as well as people often going into hidden spots in the canyon, making pools for the hot water to bathe in, and "skinny dipping" in the hot water.

Frank Fossett, early travel writer, reported in 1885 that the Colorado State Board of health had investigated the claims of hot springs in Colorado and made excellent reports about their cleanliness and curative powers, although analysis of the contents of their waters showed different results. It was noted that the Ouray springs gave off very little odor as compared to others in Colorado Springs because its sulphur content was extremely low. The State Board of Health also noted the Ridgway hot water pools (Orvis), which were then called "the Ouray Spring" after Chief Ouray who came to bathe in it often for his health problems. The pool's water was analyzed as bicarbonates, sulphur, chloride, calcium, magnesium, potassium, sodium, and as having lithium (many of these elements are still used in medicines so many of the cures probably occurred.

The hot springs, located near today's Ridgway, were evidently used for centuries by the Ute Indians and were considered both sacred and healing. The spot was so important to them that when the San Juans were sold to the United States in 1873, there was a specific provision that if the springs were found by surveyors to be on the land the Utes were selling that it would not be considered part of the sale and would remain the property of the Utes. Sure enough, when the government survey was made it showed the springs had been in the land sold but the government honored the treaty and marked the land as belonging to the Utes. One square mile of land that surround the springs and a few smaller springs in the area, were kept for a while by the Utes, but when they were forced to leave Colorado in 1880 they also gave up their rights to the hot springs.

When the whites took over Orvis hot springs, the area was called Orvis Resort and was proclaimed to have the best trout fishing in Colorado (Ouray did not have good fishing in the Uncompahgre as most of the fish in the river died). Orvis was far enough downstream for the fish to live but some said they could not reproduce at that spot in the river. Fishing there was basically in lakes and irrigation ditches. Orvis soon had an enclosed pool and log bathhouses but also had an early RV type park, a hot water heated club house, and held regular dances. Orvis had a post office from 1877 to 1879 known as the "Hot Springs" post office, even though it was on Ute land. Perhaps it was a little south of Orvis and served the north end of the valley.

LAKE LEONORE
Always A Pleasure to Visit

⁓ ⁓

There is evidence that early on Utes enjoyed the swampy little pond that was initially located where Lake Lenore is today. They evidently escaped the Uncompahgre Valley heat, hunted the plentiful game in the area, and used it as a place to keep stolen horses even before they began the rough route over Horsethief Trail. Many arrowheads, fire pits, and campsites have been found in the area.

Samuel and Sarah Mannon bought the land from the federal government in 1884. It was the Mannons that eventually built and owned three ice houses at the lake. There has always been the question of which "Lenore" the lake was named after. Many claim it was the famous "Lenore" of Edgar Allen Poe, but the first owners, the Mannons, had a daughter by that name and may have been using the name "Lenore" before selling the property. Others feel that when George Wettengel bought the property he changed the name to Lake Lenore. Wettengel at one time owned several bordellos in Ouray and is thought to have operated a similar establishment on the shores of Lake Lenore. In 1902 Mannon had leased the Lake Lenore land to Wettengel, who was one of the toughest dance hall owners in Ouray, and one of Wettengell's notorious bordellos (the Bon Ton or the Temple of Music on Second Street or both) in Ouray was so bad that the city fathers revoked his license to operate. The city licensed bordellos in the town to make sure that the girls were regularly checked by a doctor for diseases and for the good money that could be obtained for the license. The story is that two of Wettengell's most popular prostitutes were named Lenore and Julia. His naming the lake "Lake Lenore" raised trouble between the girls; however, George solved the problem by marrying Julia. During prohibition Wettengel called Lake Lenore a "country club," but it was probably more of a speakeasy.

Eventually business fell off and the place closed, probably because it was just too remote from the town (four miles). Wettengel moved back to Ouray, changed his ways, and became a respectable citizen. (Wettengel was a nephew of the well-respected and early Ouray pioneer Gus Begole, who was one of the discoverers of the Mineral Farm Mine.) After Wettengell's wife died, he would walk every day to the Cedar Hill cemetery to her grave site, usually bringing fresh flowers during season. The cemetery is located half way between Ouray and Ridgway, and is five miles each way.

Ice houses near Lake Lenore are shown in the summer of 1898.
(Ouray County Historical Society Collection)

ALLIGATORS AT THE OURAY POOL
But They Never Ate Anyone!

⁓ ⁓

The spot where the Ouray hot springs pool is now located has seen many uses over the years. At first it was a very swampy area in both the summer and in the winter, which made it obvious that hot water underlay the pool's site. The road coming into town from the north was changed to creep as it does now along the edge of the cliffs to the north in order to allow wagon traffic to cross the boggy land. After the Americans arrived a brick making plant was located at the site owned and operated by Frank Carney, who created some fairly deep holes into which the hot water seeped. Johnnie Neville also had a saloon at the north end of the spot called Johnnie Neville's First and Last Chance Saloon. There was also a lumber yard owned by S. P. Gutshall on the south end of the spot. By 1900 the area next to the lumberyard at the south end of the park was being used for a baseball diamond.

Ed Washington, a local saloonkeeper, put a two-foot alligator in the hot water pool. The alligator was a tourist souvenir he brought back from Louisiana. There was not a huge flow of hot water to the spot, but it was enough to keep the water in the ponds warm. The alligator wouldn't stay in the pool, so a wrought iron fence was built to keep the alligator from wandering off. Someone felt sorry for the little fellow, as it bellowed almost constantly, and they sent for a mate. The alligators never reproduced (no one ever checked to see if they were male and female); but they were there for about ten years, thrived in the hot water, and grew to about six feet long each. They were a very popular attraction and many photos were taken of them.

The swimming pool was built in 1926 but the alligators were such a hit that they and the gold fish were allowed to stay. However the alligators were swept into the Uncompahgre River in 1929 when a large flood hit the pool area. No one knows exactly what happened to

The alligators were at the pool site before the pool but were there with the bathers for 1½ years before being washed away in a flood.

(Author's Photo)

the alligators, but there may have been some very surprised fishermen downstream.

Besides the attraction of the alligators, there were also big horn sheep that would regularly come down to the park in the winter for its green grass (and other food fed to them by the locals and especially the railroad crews.) Some big horns still come in certain years (perhaps especially harsh winters).

Events

THE OCCUPATION OF OURAY'S SITE
By Fishermen?

⚜ ⚜

For many decades the history books recorded that the bowl that Ouray now lies in was first visited in July of 1875 by prospectors Gus Begole and Jack Eckles. They made their trip from Baker's Park, prospected up the Animas River and down the Uncompahgre. By the fall of that year they also discovered the nearby Mineral Farm vein and spent the winter of 1875-76 in the Ouray bowl, celebrating Christmas by drinking vinegar with a few other prospectors who had stayed when no whiskey could be found. Hence the name of "Vinegar Hill," now a favorite sledding spot in town. A. J. Stanley and Logan Whitlock were in the bowl fishing when they discovered the Trout and Fisherman lodes on August 23, 1875. When they returned to Bakers Park for supplies, several dozen men followed them back to Ouray and the word of mineral discoveries was out!

It was also often written that the first Americans in the interior of the San Juans were the six-man Baker party in 1860 (Baker came back the next spring with a much bigger group.) Now we know that several other groups besides Baker visited the area around Ouray in 1859-1860. One group of about a dozen men even spent the winter near Ouray in the winter of 1860-61, while Baker and his group went to Denver for the winter. R. F. Long and Captain M. W. Cline were soon in the basin. In 1875 Whitlock and Staley took ore out from the Ouray area that they sold in Mineral Point for $800. This gave them enough money to buy food and equipment that would last them all winter. It also set the stage for a major rush of prospectors to the Ouray bowl in the spring of 1876.

We also now know that mountain men such as Albert Pfieffer and Kit Carson visited the San Juans in the 1830s and reported signs of gold and silver, and that military commander Lt. William Gilpin and some of his men visited the southern San Juans in 1848, shortly after the Mexican-American War ended and the San Juans became property of the United States. Gilpin, unlike Baker, found gold but came back later and couldn't find it again. He did however tell anyone who would listen that there was gold in the San Juans.

The federal government was paid $375 for the land covered by the Ouray town site. One reason for starting the town of Ouray at this time was that Washington was moving the Los Piños Agency from Cochetopa Pass to the Uncompahgre Valley, which would bring a lot of business to the new town, as both Silverton and Lake City were about sixty miles away by the then existing route. It was not known back in the 1860s, but good mineral discoveries would also be made at the Virginius, near the south side of Mt. Sneffles and Imogene Basins and a supply town with a wagon road from the east side of the Continental Divide would be needed nearby for both of these mining camps. Otto Mears soon started a toll road from Saguache to Lake City and then from Lake City (actually the nearby little town of Barnum) to the new agency. It was rough but still a road that could be used by White settlers and merchants going to Ouray, as the existing treaty allowed roads through Ute territory.

Most of the landscape photos taken of Ouray before 1882 (when the Tabeguache Utes were removed from Colorado leaving only the Southern Ute Reservation along Colorado's southern border) show a giant United States flag flying in the middle of the town. Not one but two towering tree trunks were needed to get all of the flag off the ground. The spot became a gathering place for the people of Ouray. The flag pole was covered with notices, and a well-used speaker's platform was built about ten feet up the pole, and was especially useful on the Fourth of July. However the flag was put there only partially to show patriotism. It was mainly used to show the Utes the might of the Americans.

Ouray's location was very close to the boundary of the Ute Reservation after 1873 when the Utes sold the San Juans for $25,000 a year to be paid "forever," although after twenty years of payments the U.S. could amortize the balance and pay the balance still due forever in one lump sum. However no immediate surveys were made in the area and no one knew exactly where the boundary was in the Ouray area, other than somewhere in the valley between today's Ouray and Ridgway. The flag was meant to show prospectors coming out of the San Juan

Mountains along Cañon Creek or the Uncompahgre River that Ouray was definitely in U. S. territory and therefore could be considered a safe place to stay. A lot of the newcomers didn't care and ended up building in the Ute portion of the park.

The Ouray bowl was used for centuries by the Utes before the Americans arrived. It had game and firewood (it was heavily wooded), hot water, was relatively level, had good drinking water, and was relatively warm in the winter for the area. The plat for the original town of "Uncompahgre" was drawn and filed in 1875. "Uncompahgre" is a Ute word for "red hot water." The name is pronounced just as it is spelled Un-com-pah-gre. The Spanish had called the river the "San Francisco." During the winter of 1875-76 there two factions of prospectors, speculators, and potential citizens living in Ouray formed. There was money to be made selling town lots, and the first group that had arrived eventually formed the town council for Uncompahgre; but not to be outdone the second group formed one for Ouray. The last name came from the overall chief of the Utes and it was hoped that it would help solidify friendship with the Utes. What the new arrivals didn't realize was that although Ouray was a good friend of the Whites, many, if not most, of the Utes felt that Ouray was selling them out to the Whites and were at the point of rebellion. Many Utes complained that he was giving away their land without them even knowing it was happening. The Utes often visited the Town of Ouray, but usually it was to illegally buy liquor, gamble, or race their horses against the white man's horses for money. Only occasionally would they come to trade or to buy or sell goods.

Many of today's visitors to the city ask how to pronounce its name. The Utes had no "r" in their oral language (they had no written language) so the way they pronounced Ouray's name was more like our Oo-ay or Ou-lay in English. The Ute language is also very guttural and it is sometimes almost impossible to figure out how to write a Ute word in English. The Spanish wrote the chief's name as Ure', which would be pronounced as You-Ray. Ouray also signed his name at one time or another as Ure', Ulay, Uray, and Ouray. However since the Utes had no written language the chief was only spelling his name the way some American told him to do. The residents of the town today have pretty well settled on You-Ray, which rhymes with Hooray.

THE RIVERSIDE SNOW SLIDE
Even a Song Written About It

➤➤

The Riverside Slide has been deadly to humanity since the building of the Million Dollar Highway by Otto Mears in 1883. Before that time the road to Silverton from Ouray went up the Uncompahgre River (now the Engineer Jeep Road) to Mineral Point and then down the Animas River to Silverton. Building a road from the Engineer cut-off directly to Ironton Park was considered impossible, but Otto Mears did the impossible. His road was shorter but more dangerous. There are over 100 slides along the Million Dollar Highway and the most dangerous is well known among travelers – the Riverside Slide. Many lives have been lost in the Riverside, even though in the nineteenth

In this scene about 1888 we can see the tunnel, the stage waiting on the other side to come through, a trail on the left over the top burro and mule pack trains that would not have done well in a tunnel, and the tremendous amount of debris the slide brought down. (Author's Collection)

century a snow tunnel was usually created through the slide when the snow got deep enough. These tunnels were used later in the summer as tourist attractions and were big enough that the stage could be driven through it. By that time of year the tourists had arrived, however, the snow slides were not running.

There are 101 avalanches along both sides of the Million Dollar Highway, but it is the Riverside that is considered the most danger-ous. Dozens of people have been killed or trapped in the slide. Snow-slides have killed over sixty-five people in Ouray County. Over 200 more have been caught but survived an avalanche because their heads were above the snow or they were trapped in snow or debris pockets with enough air to last until they were rescued. Some survivors were extremely lucky. Al Look in his book *Sidelights of Colorado History* tells of two prospectors in the 1870s who were carried down a San Juan mountain by a snow slide and buried under ten or more feet of snow. It would have been impossible to dig themselves out as the snow in an ava-lanche packs like concrete and they would have suffo-cated in minutes, but before that time another slide ran, uncovered them, and left them exposed on the top of the snow.

In the days before auto-mobiles, San Juan ava-lanches were the most dangerous hazard to travel-ers – men on foot or using snowshoes or skis, or men on horseback who needed to follow packed paths, some-times with mule trains or driving burros. Quite a few

Memorial at Riverside Slide for the three snow plow drivers killed on separate occasions. Eddie Imel's name was added after the memorial was placed for the other two.

(Author's Collection)

The three crosses monument at Riverside in memory of the Rev. Marvin Hudson and his two daughters Amelia and Pauline, who all died in one slide.   Bill Fries III Photo (Author's Collection)

buildings were also hit in avalanche paths that were not recognized as such. In recent times the danger from avalanches is mainly to cross country skiers, people who have stopped in avalanche paths to put on chains or with car trouble, or to snow plow drivers who are clearing a snow slide when another slide runs in the same place. The danger is minimal to those traveling today in automobiles as long as they do not stop in an avalanche path. The avalanche paths along the major highways are clearly marked, and when in a path, keep moving, especially if there are signs that a slide might be coming. Most paths are narrow enough that a vehicle moving as slow as ten or twenty miles an hours will only be in a slide's path for a few seconds. You would have to be awfully unlucky to be in the path of a slide during the few seconds in which it could hit your vehicle.

The snowplow memorial at the Riverside Slide commemorates the lives of three brave snowplow drivers: Robert Miller (March 2, 1970), Terry Kishbaugh (February 10, 1978), and Eddie Imel (March 5, 1992). Kishbaugh's death led to the building of the snow shed, but it was much shorter than needed, so Imel still died there just outside the concrete shed. Just south of the snow shed is a memorial to the Rev. Marvin Hudson and his two daughters who were killed on March 3, 1863, when Hudson stopped in the slide's path to put chains on his tires. It took workers a week to find the body of Rev. Hudson and another week to find the body of his daughter Amelia. His daughter Pamela's body was not found for two more months.

C. W. McCall wrote a song about the Riverside Slide and the brave snow plow drivers.

> *Yeah, all a' us folks around Ouray County*
> *Seen a lota them cold, black nights*
> *When the only thing movin' is a big ol' plow*
> *Flashing them weird blue lights*
> *We found the boy in the early spring*
> *Still settin', the plow on its side*
> *Yeah, ya never quite know what time a' the night*
> *You gonna die in the Riverside Slide*

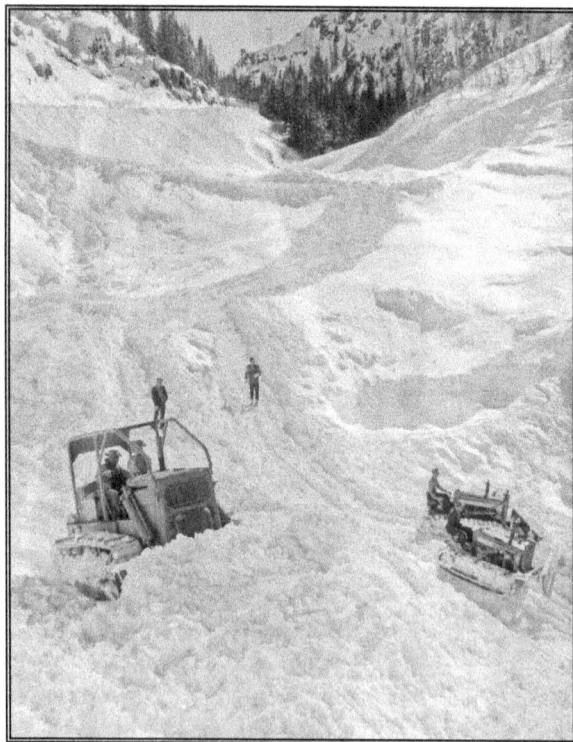

Bulldozers moving snow packed as hard as concrete trying to find the Hudson's bodies in the Riverside Slide and/or car.
(Author's Collection)

THE CUDDIGAN HANGINGS
Ouray Hangs a Pregnant Woman

There were very few hangings of women in the "Wild West," and perhaps there was only one of a pregnant woman, but such an event occurred in the City of Ouray and was accepted by the townspeople as warranted. However the town's reputation suffered greatly elsewhere in Colorado and other states. You make up your mind what you would have done.

Reports of the hanging of Mike and Margaret Cuddigan vary a little, but we will use the version of William Saunders from his newly discovered and published book *Joy of the Frontier*. The event happened in the winter of 1883-84 when Saunders was a reporter for *The Ouray Times*. In January of 1884 people began to realize that a girl of fifteen (several other sources write she was ten) who worked for the Cuddigans was no longer being seen outside. The girl, Mary Rose Matthews, was said to be their niece, and they had agreed to take her from a Catholic orphanage in Denver and brought her to their ranch seven miles south of Ouray where they grew potatoes and beans for the Ouray market.

A worried school teacher who visited the Cuddigan home on January 13, 1884, was told the little girl had died and was buried on the Cuddigan's place. However the Cuddigans would or could not say how she died and had not taken her to a doctor before she died. It was also suspected that the Cuddigan's had mistreated the girl, as two women described her shortly before her death as looking very emaciated and frightened. Saunders was invited to go with a posse that had been formed to see if there was any foul-play and he recorded the findings of the Sheriff.

The Sheriff's posse found the grave and dug up the frozen body. The Sheriff took the body out of the grave and took off her bloody frock. The body was well-preserved because of the freezing weather, and her face was bruised and her nose evidently broken. There were wide and deep cuts on her entire body. The couple was taken to Ouray and the body delivered to the local undertaker. After an examination by and testimony from the Ouray doctor, a coroner's jury ruled her death was due to cruelty, mistreatment, and inattention at the hands of the Cuddigans and Mrs. Cuddigan's brother James Carroll, who had fled the area when he heard of the posse being formed. Late that night the men of the posse joined with a few others, went to the Sheriff's house, and told the Sheriff to give them the keys to the jail (actually it was the Delmonico hotel as Ouray had no jail at the time) and they would give him no trouble. He did so (some say after a fight) and the men went to the "jail" and got the couple. The woman begged that they not hang her as she said she was six months pregnant. The men got a lantern and determined that she was in fact pregnant. A vote was taken among the men and it was unanimous to hang her. The couple was hung from different sides of a tree at the present-day ball park.

It was not long before the Denver papers picked up the story and the citizens of that town were horrified. Their criticism continued for days and the Ouray authorities finally decided to dig up the little girl's body a second time and send it to Denver to be displayed at an undertaker's office. Many Denver people saw the body and almost all agreed that the hanging was justified and appropriate. A Catholic priest from the orphanage later testified he saw the girl at Christmas and she looked okay. Instead of another disinterment of the body of the girl, a cry went out in Colorado for removal of the priest. A Grand Jury investigated and no action was taken. Matters then settled back to normal.

THE SILVER PANIC
Gold to the Forefront

➥ ➥

The San Juan's initial rush of prospectors was caused by the discovery of massive amounts of silver – so much, in fact, that the San Juans was given the nickname of "The Silvery San Juans." One great discovery after another was made until the massive Creede silver discovery in 1892. However with such large amounts of silver coming on the market, the price of silver began to slip even before the Creede discoveries.

What happened was a good example of the government trying to help matters and only making them worse. The price of silver had originally been fixed by the federal government on a ratio of one-sixteenth the price of gold. In 1878 the Bland-Allison Act required the U.S. government to purchase between two and four million dollars in silver each month. The prices of silver then rallied to $1.21 an ounce, but soon began to sink again. Then the Sherman Silver Purchase Act of 1890 required the U. S. Treasury to purchase 4.5 million ounces of silver each month, the approximate total production of all the silver mined monthly in the United States at the time. The price of silver again rallied, this time to $1.05 per ounce. Then silver prices again began to decline – this time even more steeply than ever before. The price of gold even began to fall. Then Grover Cleveland, who advocated that gold be the only monetary standard of the United States was elected President.

By 1892 a serious recession had hit the United States, silver prices were plummeting, and even more large amounts of silver was coming on the market because of the huge new discoveries of silver made at Creede. By the middle of 1893, silver prices were down to seventy-eight cents. In June the Sherman Silver Purchase Act was repealed and the price of silver fell to fifty cents an ounce. Most silver mines could not operate at a profit with silver prices so low (some of Creede's mines were exceptions) and mines began to close throughout Colorado. The resulting Colorado Depression was as bad as or worse than the Great

Depression that hit the United States in August of 1929. Many men were out of work in Ouray, as it strongly depended on silver. Railroads were going bankrupt as there was basically no ore to ship. Banks and shops shut down as mining town's citizens moved away. The Ouray paper wrote:

> It makes one's heart bleed to pass through the once fair and thrifty city (of Ironton), and take note of the ravages of time. Handsome business houses with their doors and windows boarded up, stand as monuments of the terrible crime of '93. Dwelling houses falling into decay... water works unused and gone to rack and ruin, with water from their mains gushing up in the roads. Everything seems to have gone to seed.
>
> Ouray-Silverite-Plaindealer, *February 2, 1894.*

Ouray could have become a ghost town, except for a few factors – gold had been discovered near Ouray at the American Nettie, and some of the Ouray mines had such high grade silver that they could still operate profitably. Still, Ouray's citizens had a cruel and uncertain future, but they were not going to panic, pick up their belongings, and move on. Instead they stayed and rededicated themselves to their town. Out of work miners became prospectors and placer miners began searching for gold in the rivers and creeks. Tourism was also beginning to take off in Ouray. The Million Dollar Highway, The Rio Grande Southern Railroad, and the Silverton Railroad all helped. Then in 1896 Tom Walsh discovered the high grade gold veins of the Camp Bird Mine. Gold had regularly showed up in the local smelter reports but many smelters would not pay for less than an ounce of gold in a ton of ore. Some smelters were now breaking that rule. The March 2, 1894 paper announced "Ouray will have a gold boom the coming summer." Ouray was saved!

EARLY FOURTH OF JULY CELEBRATIONS
Wild, Wooly, and Long

~ ~

One of the favorite events of the year in Ouray has always been the Fourth of July, but today's activities are nothing compared to those of the late 1800s and early 1900s. Miners and prospectors poured out of the hills to enjoy what was usually a three-day celebration. The event included all of those we usually see today, but many more. The stores and houses were all decorated for the celebration with very few exceptions.

The day usually started with cases of dynamite being set off at midnight. The resulting concussion would often break out dozens of windows in town. Many times Ouray also had "shooting anvils" which were blacksmith anvils whose holes were filled with black powder and lit. Ouray had its water fights but the water system had small pebbles in it in those days and participants often came away bleeding and in some cases the water fight even had to be stopped because of the bad physical condition of a participant. Speakers talked almost constantly in different parts of town and everyone had an American flag. The races included foot races, sack races, three legged races, burro races, horse races, and firemen's hose cart races—all the contests were heavily bet on. There were contests to see who could catch a greased pig or climb a greased pole. There were rock drilling contests that had very large cash prizes, sometimes $500 or $1,000, small fortunes in those days. Manually drilling a twenty-four inch hole into hard granite in fifteen minutes or less using hand drills and sledge hammers really thrilled the crowds. One man would hold the drill, while another hit it with the sledge, then the man holding the drill rotated it and it was hit again with the sixteen pound sledge. After a set time the men would change places, usually without missing a beat or hitting the other man with the sledge. The same action was necessary when switching to longer steel drills as the holes deepened.

An early Ouray Fourth of July parade approaching the large city flagpole from the north. Evidently the town's militia is at the bottom center as the men all carry rifles.   (Author's Collection)

There were also contests to see who could pack three one hundred pound bags of ore on a mule and run with them a short distance to show the bags would not fall off. Winners of these contests were often eligible to then enter state or national contests with even bigger prizes.

There were prize fights, balls at different places in town, baseball tournaments, balloon ascensions, and pigeon and turkey shoots. A formal ball was held at the Beaumont and there was also a less casual dance at Wright's Opera House, and of course many of the miners were whooping it up in the saloons and dance halls.

Excursion trains pulling six or seven cars were used to allow towns people from the nearby valleys to visit their favorite mining town. The Ouray parades included all kinds of elaborate floats. Bands played, State Guard units marched in their full dress uniforms and played their instruments. Fireworks went off during the day and night.

OURAY'S SEMI-PRO BASEBALL TEAM
Including Smoky Joe Woods

~~~ ~~~

Minor league baseball was a major event in Ouray at the beginning of the twentieth century. Virtually every Colorado town had a semi-pro team and excursion trains with special rates would take a town's fans to away games. Silverton residents came to Ironton by train and then down to Ouray by stagecoach. Ouray had some very competitive games, especially with Telluride and Silverton. Competition became so keen that Ouray once paid a professional team from Montana to play for them and eventually was the winner of the season's series with the other two San Juan towns.

A lumber yard had opened near today's baseball field, but after a few years it closed and moved to Delta. About 1900 the shed that had been used for the lumber was converted into covered stands for spectators,

Ouray's baseball field was used before the pool was built and the old lumberyard sheds seen here in the middle were used for spectator seating. The fishpond is in the foreground.   (Author's Collection)

but baseball ceased during World War I and the field was planted with potatoes (which did not do well). About 1920 baseball and the baseball field were revived.

Some of Ouray's players eventually made it to the major league. Smoky Joe Woods was one of those players. Smoky Joe Woods played two years in Ouray – as a fourteen and fifteen year-old pitcher on the Ouray team. If you have never heard of Smoky Joe then you are not a baseball fan or at least not a baseball historian. His actual name was Howard Ellsworth Wood but his father called him Joe and the "Smoky" came from his blazing fastball. Wood was born in Kansas City, Kansas, but came to Colorado Springs in 1899 at the age of nine. The family soon moved to Ouray where they lived for five or six years.

Some say Smoky Joe was the greatest pitcher in U. S. history of all time, but only during his relatively short career with the Boston Red Socks (1908-1915) and the Cleveland Indians (1917 to 1922 and during which time he was injured). He had broken his thumb while pitching and had a very sore arm that forced his early retirement and even earned him the phrase "Smoky Joe Syndrome," which in baseball lingo means a player with unbelievable talent and who should be in the baseball hall of fame, but whose career was cut short by injuries. Joe's statistics included a 117-57 won-loss record, a 2.03 earned run average, 989 strikeouts, and a .283 batting average. Woods once struck out fifteen batters in a row, pitched a no hitter in 1911, had the major league record for most wins in 1912 and the best earned run average in 1915. Even though his injuries shortened his career, he is usually included in baseball lists of the 100 greatest players of all time. And he pitched for the Ouray team for two years!

Smoky Joe Wood's actual name was Howard Wood but his father nicknamed him Joe after a former clown he met at the Kansas State Fair. The "Smoky" came from Joe's fast ball.

(Author's Collection)

THE MOVIES
"True Grit, "How the West Was Won," and More

⟋ ⟋

Ouray County's scenery is amazing and it hasn't escaped the notice of the movie industry. *True Grit* (1969), *How the West Was Won* (1962), *Across the Great Missouri* (1951), *Butch Cassidy and the Sundance Kid* (1969), *Tribute to a Bad Man* (1956), and several dozen other movies have been filmed, at least in great part, in Ouray County. Numerous television shows and documentaries have also been filmed in Ouray.

The 1962 film *How The West Was Won* was filmed in part in the Cow Creek area of Ouray County. Henry Hathaway was the film's producer and was exposed to the true beauty of Ouray County during this time, and when he was picked to produce the epic film *True Grit* he insisted that it be filmed in Ouray County instead of Ft. Smith, Arkansas, where the movie was supposed to take place. *True Grit* was perhaps the most famous film made in Ouray County and one of the most recent as it was filmed in 1969. It is also famous for being the first film to earn superstar western actor John Wayne his first Oscar.

How the West Was Won (1962) was an epic western that was filmed across the United States and was set in the years 1839 to 1889. Its cast included over a dozen big name stars including Henry Fonda, Gregory Peck, Walter Brennan, George Peppard, Robert Preston, Debbie Reynolds, James Stewart, and John Wayne. Ridgway's old railroad station (now a private residence) was used in the movie as The Independence Hotel. Scenes from Courthouse Mountain and from along Last Dollar Road (accessed at Dallas Divide) were also used in both movies. Debbie Reynolds loved the Cow Creek area so much that she bought a large ranch there where her mother lived for many years, often visited by Debbie Reynolds.

John Wayne and the film crew almost took over Ouray and Montrose Counties during its filming and many of the locals were used as extras in the film. The Ouray County courthouse and the nearby Mineral Farm Mine had scenes that were prominent in the film, Ouray's courthouse being used for the opening courtroom scene and the "snake pit" scenes being filmed at the Mineral Farm. The business district of the town of Ridgway was totally transformed by Montrose artist Bob DeJulio into what was supposed to be an early Arkansas town. The Ridgway Visitor's Center still gives tours pointing out which local buildings and spots were used in the film. Paramount Pictures in 2007 came back to Ouray County and filmed the various spots where the film was shot as a documentary called *Aspen Gold: The Locations of True Grit*. There was also a new *True Grit* in 2010 that followed the same plot but which was filmed mainly in Texas and New Mexico and which starred Jeff Bridges and Hailee Steinfeld.

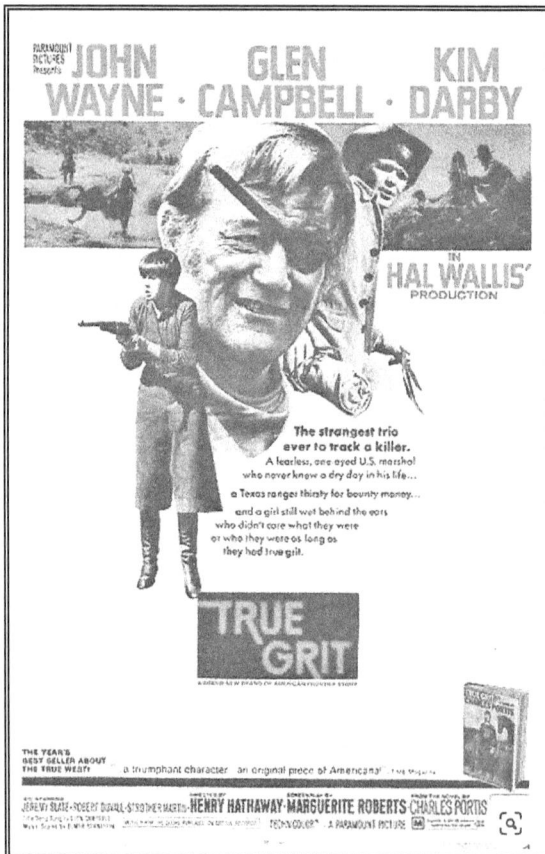

This True Grit *poster highlights actors John Wayne, Glen Campbell, and Kim Darby.* (Author's Collection)

THE BUILDING OF OURAY'S HOT SPRING POOL
A Community Effort

Ouray's present Community Pool was not the first in Ouray. It was not until 1914 that a petition was circulated and money collected to allow the city to buy the land for a swimming pool, baseball diamond, and playground. The city cleaned up the area, built a gazebo, and established a picnic area, but no pool was built. In 1923 the already existing Ouray Recreation Association took over the task of constructing a hot springs pool. The money was raised, a two year construction project undertaken and by 1925 a 150 by 280 oval pool that was two to ten feet deep had been built. The hot springs pool originally cost only $35,000 because of the volunteer efforts of many in the community, and at the time it was built it was one of the largest pools in the United States.

The pool would hold over a million gallons of water, but no one had checked to see how much hot water was available for use at the pool. Unfortunately an extensive search in the area around the pool produced "only a small trickle of hot water." For a year the pool sat empty. Eventually enough hot water was located near Box Canyon (540 gallons a minute from three different hot springs) and a pipeline was built for over a mile to the pool, which finally opened in late 1927. There was to be a bath house built at the same time but there was not enough money, so ten log cabanas with canvas tops (locally called the "cabanas") were substituted. The pool did well in 1928; but then in 1929, not only did the stock market crash, but a major flood in July caused the Uncompahgre River to sweep the cabanas into the pool, fill the pool with dirt, rocks and other debris, and washed the gold fish and alligators down the river. In the spring of 1930 volunteers dug out the debris and built a true bath house. Materials for the bath house were furnished by businesses that agreed to wait for payment until the city was capable of paying. The Recreation Association deeded the pool to the city at this time and over the next few years the pool was leased to individuals who wished to run it for a portion of its profits. During the 1930s the WPA also channeled the course of the Uncompahgre River through the town, which expanded the ballpark and other facilities and helped protect the pool from further flooding of the river. The goldfish ponds were reduced in size to one pond but restocked.

It was at this time that the city pool joined other locations in town and advertised its pool as having been proven by government analysis "to be the most radioactive on the North American continent." It was a gross exaggeration but was widely publicized, including by the D&RG Railroad. The pool was especially touted as relieving arthritis and rheumatism. Visitors were also encouraged to drink the water and the claim was made that the springs "were almost as famous as the fountain of perpetual youth for keeping or regaining health." It was not until 1976 that the pool was opened for winter use on a regular basis, which had only been done sporadically before that time. The

Only a year after it was built the pool and baseball field flooded and the dressing cabanas were washed away. It was a year before the mess was cleaned up and a new bath house built. The D&RG train can be seen on the other side of the river.   (Author's Collection)

pool recently underwent a major remodeling and it is hoped it will be enjoyed for many years to come.

An overview of the Ouray pool shortly after being restored after the flood shows the river channelized, a new bathhouse, and a large gold fish pond.
(Author's Collection)

TODAY'S ICE CLIMBING
A Wonderful Compliment to the Hot Springs

❦ ❦

Back in the mid-to-late- 1970s, at the time the author and his family moved to Ouray, the mining that the town had relied on for over a hundred years began to come to an end. As the miners began to move away, a large number of new people began to move to the town. Housing prices were very affordable, but the question from the younger people was "How do we make a living here?" It was a question that had or would eventually be heard in all the San Juan mining towns. Summer tourism was one answer, but there was too short a season for locals to make enough to live in town all year. Various committees were formed, festivals were started, much money was spent on advertising, and finally the hot springs pool was configured to open in the winter. That action eventually made business in the winter viable, but the residents didn't stop there.

A major water line ran along the Uncompahgre Canyon in Ouray to a hydroelectric plant that had been used off and on for years. The water came from a dam several miles upriver and by the 1980s the pipeline was leaking in several places. In the winter those leaks became huge icicles. A few people had climbed the ice of various San Juan waterfalls in the winter for the excitement, but several Ouray locals envisioned an ice park in Ouray and solicited the cooperation of the owner of the hydroelectric plant, who also had an easement for the pipeline from the dam to the hydroelectric plant. The City of Ouray was also willing to give the idea a try. A lot of experimentation went into to the ice park one sees today; but eventually Ouray was known for its tremendous ice climbing park and another attraction was born for the winter economy. It also dovetailed perfectly with the hot springs pool – hot and cold action in the winter.

The ice climbing park currently has over a mile of vertical terrain and over 200 separate climbs for ice and rock climbers of all abilities.

Every winter the Ouray Ice Festival, the largest of its kind in the world, draws thousands of visitors and raises funds to keep the ice park free to the public.

The ice park is located within Box Canyon Park, which is perhaps the oldest and most visited natural attraction of Ouray. If ice climbing isn't your sport you will find a visit to Box Canyon Falls to be just as exciting and a lot less dangerous. Canyon Creek has worn more than 200 feet through the rock across the ages by the twisting and turning water of its waters. The city (for a small fee) allows visitors to walk inside the grotto

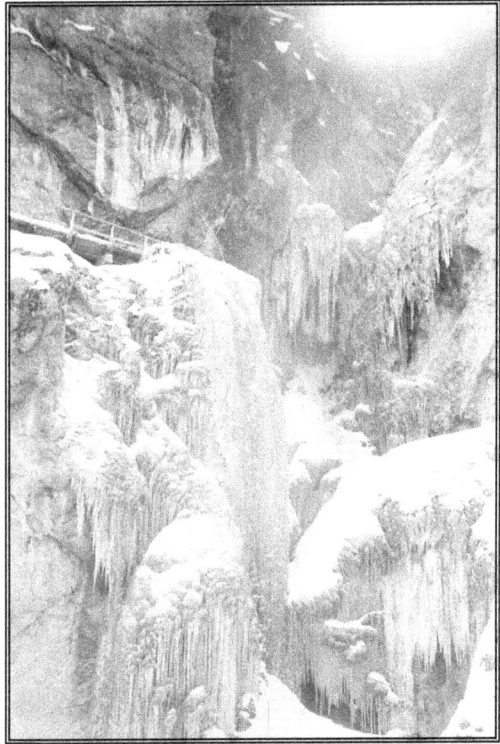

Box Canyon has always been a winter wonderland of ice, but was not officially encouraged for ice climbing. Instead the ice park was eventually formed in the nearby Uncompahgre Canyon.

(Author's Collection)

along a path and catwalk to the very base of the falls. The electric company blasted out the route in the late 1890s to allow a pipeline for water to its hydroelectric plant on the Uncompahgre. In the summer it is a favorite area for tourists to cool off. In the winter the chamber becomes a fairyland of ice.

The park is open mid- to late-December to mid-March, 8:00 a.m. to 4 p.m. depending on weather conditions. Climbers need crampons and helmets. Guides and rental equipment can be found at local sports stores. Please make yourself aware of and follow the park's rules. All risks, known and unknown are yours.

A CHILD'S FIRST BURRO
Like Today's Teenager's First Car

~~ ~~

Burros became a favorite riding animal for women and children because they were so gentle and being so close to the ground a fall from a burro by a woman riding side-saddle or a child wasn't as dangerous as one from a taller horse or mule. Burros were everywhere in the San Juans and every town had its favorite burros and its favorite burro tales, as it seemed they were always getting into trouble or performing some heroic deed. Women did however get upset when burros would come into their yards and eat their flowers or sometimes even the

An early day birthday party for a child living on Oak Street was made complete with a burro ride.   (Author's Collection)

clothes off their clothes lines. Some burros were said to even know how to unlatch a gate to get into a yard.

Children especially loved burros, some even using them for the apex of their see-saws. Having your own burro was somewhat like a young adult of today getting his first car. Best of all the animals could usually be found roaming loose and could be obtained for free if the owner had left town. Burros became not only a mode of transportation for children but also a loving pet, as burros love kids. Sometimes a burro would even get into the family photograph like a dog sometimes does today.

Burros are especially gentle and not stubborn like many people think – they are simply very careful and perfect for a child. In the early days Ouray was full of burros that were free for the taking after being abandoned by prospectors. (Author's Collection)

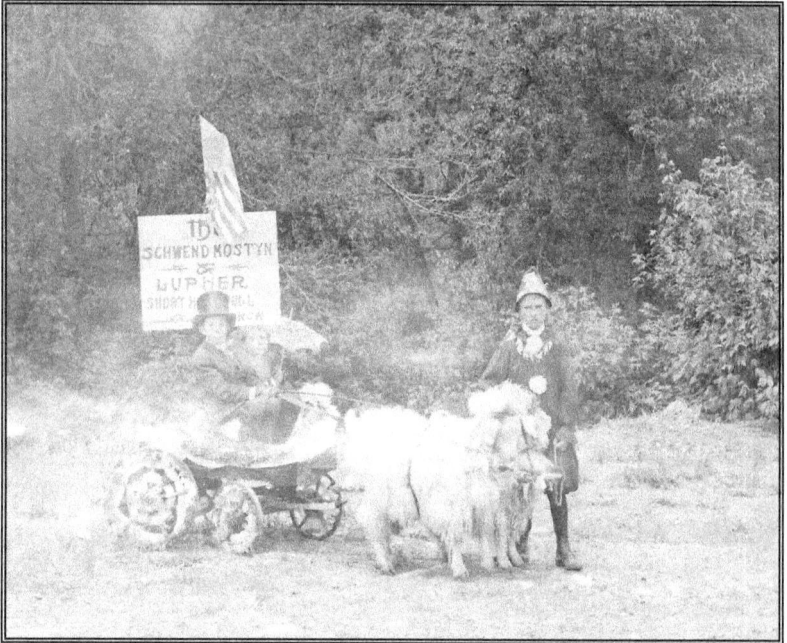

The children used not only burros but goats for transportation. A Ouray grocery store sponsored this early day Fourth of July float. Goat carts were popular at the time.   (Author's Collection)

Transportation

How the Million Dollar Highway got Its Name
Hint: It Did Not Cost Nearly $1 Million

~ ~

Most people who drive the Million Dollar Highway (technically only from Ouray to Silverton, but sometimes the term is used for the road from Ouray all the way to Durango) ask how the highway got its name. The most common of the various scenarios given is that discarded mill tailings from the local mines were used to surface the original road, and that over a million dollars in gold and silver was mixed in with the tailings. In fact no mine tailings were used at all. It is also preposterous that educated mine and mill owners would have not recognized the value of the material. One of the craziest stories is that a woman came over the highway and hysterically reported in Ouray that she would not go back over the road for a Million Dollars. The author once had a lady in his Ouray store that made that exact comment and it turned out she was talking about the road from Ridgway to Ouray. We told her she should definitely *not* go any further south. The highway also did not cost a million dollars to build – only about $125,000 – but that was an enormous sum for a road at that time.

Another reason for doubting these stories is that the road did not carry the name "The Million Dollar Highway" until the 1920s – almost forty years after it was built by Otto Mears and his crews. In the meanwhile the road did have names (the people of the day were often giving names to their roads rather than using highway numbers like we do today), in this case "The Chief Ouray Highway, The Rainbow Route, and the DSO (Durango- Silverton- Ouray) Highway were some of the names. But at no time before the 1920s was "The Million Dollar Highway" used.

The actual reason for the naming of the road was that in the 1920s automobiles were becoming popular and Colorado automobile tourism was beginning to blossom. The section of Highway 550 between Ouray and Silverton had a major upgrade at this time, including grading, widening, and even making it two lanes wide in many places. The three road contractors hired for the job were each given a specific section of road to work on and the first time they got together they compared bids and realized the three bids totaled exactly one million dollars. One of the contractors exclaimed, "Well, I guess we have ourselves a million dollar highway." A few days later a sign went up so designating the highway and the name stuck.

Many locals think the name is now not appropriate as it could today cost perhaps billions to construct and there is much more than a million dollars of scenery along the road. Still the road today continues to evoke the comment that someone wouldn't go back over it for a million dollars.

The highway from Ouray to Silverton was really scary until it was upgraded in the 1920 and received the name "The Million Dollar Highway."
(Author's Collection)

THE D&RG'S
CIRCLE ROUTE STAGE
It Was Used By Tourists From Around the World

The "Circle Route" was a promotion of the D&RG Railroad shortly after the completion of the Silverton Railroad from Ironton to Silverton in mid-1889. The Silverton Railroad extended the D&RG route but it was still a dead end. A stage took passengers from Ironton on into Ouray. In August 1893 the D&RG took over possession as receiver of the Rio Grande Southern Railroad that ran from Ridgway to Durango. This created a huge loop on D&RG track from Denver or Pueblo over to and all the way around the San Juan Mountains. It was a trip of about a thousand miles through some of the most exotic and rugged territory in the United States. The D&RG advertised the loop as "the most fantastic scenery in the world," and most of the people who took the trip agreed. The trip was relatively inexpensive (twenty-five to thirty dollars) and passengers could get off and spend a few days at any of the towns along the way at no extra charge, as long as they finished the tour in thirty days. The use of the small narrow gauge locomotives and cars was another attraction. Tourism was doing well by this time in Colorado and the trip was very popular. Ouray was on the route as a short ten mile side trip and even though the railroad dead-ended there the town benefited greatly from the Circle Route.

Before the Silver Crash of 1893 Otto Mears wanted to build a cog and/or electric railroad for the route between Ironton and Ouray, to make a complete circle (Ouray, Ridgway, Telluride, Durango, Silverton, and back to Ouray and Ridgway) by railroad. Plans were drawn in 1891 and the route surveyed along a seven percent route with several tunnels. The construction would have been very expensive, eliminated the road in many places, and perhaps the grade was just too steep, so neither a cog nor an electric railroad was ever built.

The Circle Route Concord stage originally ran on a route from the Beaumont Hotel (or sometimes the St. Elmo Hotel) in Ouray to the

The Circle Route Stage is picking up the last of its passengers in front of the St. Elmo Hotel in 1923 and other tourists are bidding them a good trip. It was truly "An Echo From the Past."   (Author's Collection)

Silverton Railroad station in Ironton. After the Silverton Railroad shut down regular passenger service in 1893, the D&RG continued to run the Circle Route Stage from Ouray to the D&RG railroad depot in Silverton. If a passenger did not want to ride on the stage (and most did) he could stay on the railroad train for the entire Circle Route which now went from Ridgway to the D&RG station at Durango and back to Denver. It was confusing but both the Ridgway-Silverton and the Ridgway-Durango routes were open.

Not only did passengers swarm to the stagecoach because of the nostalgia involved, but the Circle Route Stage often in good weather offered an open wagon for passengers called a "bus," and the D&RG continued to run the route in one form or another until automobiles could use the Million Dollar Highway in the 1920s. The stages were drawn by four to six huge horses. The choicest seats on the Concord stage were up top over the coach which made for a great view along the highway and one favored passenger usually got to ride beside the driver. Passengers in the early summer also usually got a ride through the snow tunnel at the Riverside Slide, and passengers could also get off at Red Mountain Town and spend some time in a real live mining camp.

The "Stubborn" Burros
Tails & Tales

⤚ ⤙

urros were the favorite pack animals of most of the prospectors and even some of the freighters in the San Juan Mountains. There were many reasons why they were so popular. They didn't need special grains, grass, or hay, and would eat almost anything, just like a goat. They were very sure-footed in the mountains, as unlike a horse or mule their hooves are soft and somewhat pliable. They are very sociable and were a companion that could be taken along by a prospector like a dog, although he usually took both of them. Burros could carry as much weight as a horse and almost as much as a mule, and they cost less than half as much to buy. There were even tales of burros helping prospectors find gold, usually when the men were out looking for their burro

Burros were often used to get mine rail (20 pounds per yard) or lumber, especially to mines that had no road to their operation. This photo was before 1886 as there is no Beaumont Hotel.

(Author's Collection)

that had strayed off. Nicholas Creede said he struck it rich at the "Holy Moses Mine in Creede while trying to drive a stake into the ground to tie his burro to. Because burros were cheap to buy, many prospectors simply let their burros go free to become wild when a man decided to leave the San Juan Mountains. Because they were so sure-footed burros could operate in snow too deep for mules or horses; and burros were also often used to break a trail for these other animals. Some men even made snowshoes for burros out of leather and boards and taught certain animals to operate on them; and, with or without the snow shoes, prospectors often used a technique called "tailing, where their burro broke trail and the prospector held on the burro's trail to pull him through the deep snow.

Famous western photographer William Henry Jackson shot a typical Ouray burro train ready for a new mining prospect. Their load includes a stove and a blacksmith's bellow.   (Author's Collection)

A Fight Caused by the D&RG Railroad
Ouray Almost Became A Ghost Town

By 1880 the City of Ouray was desperate for a railroad. Local smelt-ers were not working well in the high altitude of the San Juans, and it was hundreds of miles by wagon to get Ouray ores to the closest efficient smelters at Cañon City or Pueblo. There were closer smelters located in Lake City and Silverton, but their early runs were recovering only 50% or less of the valuable minerals, and the trip could not be made by wagons. The costs of bringing supplies in and ore out by wagon over the Otto Mears toll road was still very high because of the length of the trip (almost 300 miles to Pueblo). When the D&RG Railroad arrived in Montrose in 1882 and headed tracks in the direction of Ouray there was great hope of the railroad's quick arrival; however, the main route went on to Utah, and unfortunately the rails moving toward Ouray soon stopped a few miles short of today's Ridgway at the small town of Dallas. At that point it looked like the D&RG would build on to Telluride, Rico, and Durango. The Ouray mines and their ores seemed to be forgotten and those shipping by railroad had to bring their wagons through Ouray and down ten or twelve miles to Dallas.

If the minerals came from a mine with a concentrating mill, the ore was shipped in bags, and freight costs were lowered because the waste rock had been eliminated from the shipment, but still not to the point that most Ouray ore could be shipped economically to the smelters. Ouray had only a "Sampling Works" (Munn Brothers) which allowed the value of the local ores to be estimated, but there was no mill or smelter at all in Ouray. When the bonanza at Red Mountain mines was discovered in 1883, that area, which was located almost an equal distance from Ouray and Silverton, seemed it might be one of the major Colorado mining districts, rivaling even Leadville. Ouray's citizens wanted the ore to be shipped out by way of their town and supplies taken back from Ouray in the empty wagons. However the D&RG was coming into Silverton from the south and that town was likely to and did eventually get most of the Red Mountain business. Ouray needed a railroad!

At this point Dave Day of the *Solid Muldoon* came into the picture. He bought two farms about four miles north of Ouray, then founded a town site, suggesting that the mines ship by wagon through the narrow canyon from Ouray and use the new town as the end of the railroad track. Better yet, there was a small smelter (Windham) already located only about a mile from the new site and, although it was also very inefficient, the company that owned it was taking the opportunity to expand and improve their operation. Day advertised town lots for sale in the new town, eventually called "Portland," but only after the names "Dayton," "Helena," "Ramona," and "Chipeta" were considered, and he put D&RG representatives on the town site board, so that they could share in the profits from selling lots. Portland was located at the spot where the railroad would be forced to blast through the narrow canyon to get to Ouray, a very expensive proposition. Day announced that lots would be sold as soon as a survey was finished.

David Moffatt took over at this time as President of the D&RG Railroad. Moffat was a good friend of Day's and agreed to come to Portland to look over the situation. There was nothing short of great fear among Ouray businessmen, who could and would, if necessary, move their locations to Portland to be near the railroad. The residents of the town of Ouray were almost hysterical as they felt their town would become a ghost town! Then Day announced in July that Portland would be the terminus not only for Ouray, but also for the new D&RG route to be built to Telluride and Rico (Otto Mears eventually built the Rio Grande Southern on this route but from Ridgway). Then Day published a list of thirty businesses that had already bought lots in Portland.

Moffat eventually came to Portland to see what was going on for himself, but he also went to Ouray to look at the possibilities there. He went to a regularly scheduled Board of Trade meeting in Ouray and talked with many of the Ouray businessmen. When Ouray businessmen saw that the railroad might not be built to their town, they were willing to do almost anything to assure that the railroad would come. He finally agreed that if Ouray would grade, excavate, and pay for the railroad from Portland to Ouray, and if Ouray would buy the land and build the depot in town that he would extend the rails themselves at D&RG cost to Ouray. A deal was made, Day was furious (and eventually forced to leave Ouray), and Ouray's citizens could breathe easy again. No one is exactly sure what made Moffat change his mind, but he may well have received some "extra" money from the townspeople.

The tracks would be laid on the opposite (west) side of the Uncompahgre River from Portland where they would miss most of the hardrock cliffs on the east side. The railroad arrived in Ouray on December 21, 1887, and did not pass through or near Portland. The merchants and citizens of Ouray were furious that Dave Day and a few others who had worked against them in this plot to make Day and the others rich but destroying Ouray. Virtually all of the Ouray merchants stopped their advertising with the *Solid Muldoon* and instead became customers of the *Ouray Times*. Day was soon forced to move his newspaper to Durango.

The town of Portland shortly after it was learned the D&RG Railroad was not coming. It was all downhill from this point on.

(Author's Collection)

EARLY MAIL CARRIERS
They Literally Risked Their Lives to Snowstorms,
Avalanches, and Floods

In the winter time, travel was almost always difficult in the San Juans, but the old adage of "the mail must go through" was followed. In 1875 Otto Mears was given the longest (and most lucrative) mail contract in the San Juans – 150 miles from Lake City to the new Ute Indian Agency in the Uncompahgre Valley (which supplied mail to the new town of Ouray). When the winter snows got deep Mears resorted to the use of dog sleds to get the mail through and keep his contract. He hired a prospector, Stewart Daniels, who had worked for the Hudson Bay Company in Canada, to carry the mail in the winter along the new toll road using a sled pulled by dogs. The mail carrier was not supposed to ride on the sled but rather skied alongside on "Norweigan Snowshoes – basically the same as today's skis except up to ten or even twelve feet long. Since the driver (and often his dogs) would sometimes sit on top of the sled to rest, Ouray women were upset that their hats and other delicate items were often being delivered smashed. The women complained and by late winter the driver quit. To keep his contract after his dog sled driver quit and the snow was still deep in March, Otto Mears supposedly strapped the mail on his back in Lake City and carried it the 150 miles to the new Los Piños Agency. He kept the contract.

U. S. Mail carriers in the rugged and high San Juan Mountains themselves could not use the sleds, but wore web skis or what we today call snowshoes. The mail carriers from Silverton to Ouray or Lake City used such a setup. The mailmen would also often carry supplies for the isolated San Juan towns or mines along the way that were being worked all winter. If needed, the mailmen sometimes carried fifty pound sacks of flour or other heavy items strapped to their backs over some of the steepest and hairiest trails in the United States and at times when the passes were thought impassable.

The mail was very important to the locals and also very lucrative for the mail contractors. It was often the only connection of the mining camps with the outside world in the winter. People were drawn immediately to the post office to seek a letter or package, and newspapers were torn into pieces so that everyone could read the news. One trick among residents who absolutely needed to travel in bad weather was to go with the mail carrier. He would almost always get you there safe.

One mail trip that did not turn out well was by a young Swede Nelson. It was December 23, 1883, and he had the job of getting the mail from Silverton to Ophir over Ophir Pass. It was snowing hard and avalanches were running, but he felt an obligation to get the mail to Ophir because he knew his pouch contained Christmas gifts and money. He left in a total blizzard on his long wooden skis, but didn't show up at Ophir. Many thought that since he was young, he had skipped out with the money and presents. Several years went by with no one knowing of his whereabouts. Two and one half years later, in August, his brother found his body starting to thaw out of a huge avalanche. He still had the mail pouch strapped to his back. Swede had given his life in an attempt to get the Christmas mail through. Several other mail carriers with the same dedication died in avalanches in the San Juan Mountains.

The post office department in those early days was often requested to formally establish an office in some pretty small and often dangerous places, and usually they complied – at least until they saw the place was just too small. By 1876 the mail was being delivered sporadically to Ouray but the town did not get its first post office with *daily* mail until July 1878. That same summer Ouray got telephone service, but the telephone service only covered the area of the San Juans and was not yet available in other parts of Colorado. Remember the Ute Indians were still on their reservations so the postman went that way unless he wanted to go over the mountains between Lake City and Ouray. Mail usually went to Ouray and then by the Mears toll road to Lake City. From there it went to Alamosa where it was transferred to the D&RG Railroad and went to Denver. The running time to get the mail from Ouray to Alamosa was thirty-six hours.

Mail not only came into Ouray but also went out to mining camps in the area – including Sneffels, Camp Bird, Ash, Guston, Ironton,

Red Mountain Town, and the Virginius Mine at over 13,000 feet elevation. There were post offices at Sneffles and in Imogene Basins (probably at Richardson's Cabin) in 1877. And the USPS, along with many volunteers who also carried the mail when no official carrier was available, did a very good job in all kinds of weather and to very remote places. The old adage about the mail must go through seems to have been forgotten today.

Delivery of the mail in the San Juans in the winter could be a dangerous occupation.

(From *Croffut's Grip Sack Guide to Colorado*)

THE MELDRUM TUNNEL
Short Cut to Telluride

ndrew Meldrum was one of the original discoverers of the Yankee
Girl Mine at Red Mountain on August 16, 1882. The Yankee
Girl was the biggest and best of the Red Mountain mines and made
over 100 million dollars in today's values. However the four original
discoverers sold the mine for $125,000 – to be split four ways but
still a large amount in those days ($37,500 each). However Andy,
like most good prospectors, kept on searching for another bonanza,
although he bought a ranch near Delta, Colorado, where he spent
much of the winter.

After the 1893 Silver Crash several major efforts were made to
keep the Red Mountain District open. It was known that there was
still silver to be mined there, but the price of silver was so low that
it could not be economically mined unless costs were reduced drasti-
cally. Otto Mears, the D&RG, and many others had a dream that the
Silverton Railroad that ran from Silverton to Red Mountain would
be extended north to Ouray so as to make a loop and tie in with the
D&RG in Ouray. Both the D&RG and Otto Mears eventually gave
up; but Andy Meldrum had a slightly different dream. He proposed
a 24,200 foot tunnel that would run from near the town of Ironton
close to the northern end of the Red Mountain Mining District to
Telluride. The tunnel would be sufficiently large to allow the passage
of a narrow gauge locomotive and with a grade low enough to allow
the locomotive to pull a good many narrow gauge ore cars through
the tunnel, which would also be wide enough to allow a good-size
ditch to run alongside the track that would drain the large amount
of water that was expected along the way. The water would in turn
run an electric generator that would supply electricity for the entire
tunnel. Meldrum also hoped to crosscut unknown but highly possible
veins of ore that might be encountered along the way, including the

veins of some existing rich mines at lower levels than they were then able to mine.

The Meldrum Tunnel – a six mile narrow gauge railroad tunnel that would be several thousand feet under Lookout, Ajax, and Hayden Mountains was meant to access rich gold veins in the Telluride area as well as some of Red Mountain's veins. The tunnel would have a high spot near the middle to drain the water that was plaguing all the local mines and use the water to generate electricity, which could be sold to the local mines. It was expected that the tunnel would start hitting rich ore within 2,000 feet on both sides. Meldrum predicted that the project would provide a profit of $650,000 a year for many years to come. The railroad also meant ore could be shipped directly to the mills or smelters from where it was mined, thereby dropping transportation costs greatly. Meldrum went to Scotland to find the funds he needed for his project and, because the project sounded so reasonable, he was able to soon raise enough money to start the project. He estimated he would need another three million dollars to finish and that the project would take six years. Unfortunately the Boer War broke out in Africa and cut off Meldrum's financial support, so the tunnel was never finished.

However in 1947-1948 the Idarado Mining Company bought the unfinished Meldrum Tunnel on the Telluride side and they discovered several rich veins near that area. They extended the Meldrum tunnel in a smaller form and completed a 600 foot raise inside the mountain that connected Telluride and their mine on Red Mountain (the old Treasury Tunnel), which allowed them to take Ouray ore to their mill in Telluride. This then made it possible to use the tunnel and their mine as a major shortcut between the two sides, but Andy's larger tunnel and railroad were never finished.

Technically you would only be in the Meldrum tunnel today if you enter on the Telluride side where the tunnel is eight feet high and ten feet wide – a size big enough for a narrow gauge train. This is still private property, owned by the Idarado Mine, but every now and then a tour is given. This part of the tunnel was at one time a nuclear fallout shelter for the Town of Telluride! On what is called "The Mill Level" the Meldrum Tunnel begins at 9,062 feet and gradually rises and is now about 2 ½ miles into Ajax Mountain to drain water from the mine. The Idarado is entered at 10,600 feet on the Red Mountain side, but it is not the Meldrum Tunnel, which is much lower down towards Ironton Park. This access (the Treasury Tunnel) was started about fifty years ago and barely had room for the little mining locomotive that takes miners in.

Within the nearby mountains there are hundreds of miles of old workings of many different claims that the Idarado bought. The Idarado still owns most of the claims and the old mill, but is now doing only rehab work to keep the tunnels open in case the price of gold goes high enough to again begin production. The mill's main job today is to keep the quality of the water coming out of the mine acceptable to the EPA. If the mine were to get approval to open again, ore chutes would be tunneled to connect with some of the existing big mines in the area.

Another purpose of the Meldrum Tunnel was to drop the costs of mining so low that even low grade ore would be economical to mine and ship to the smelters. A lot of that low grade ore is still there and is now more valuable with the rise in metal prices. It was also hoped that some rich veins might be discovered during the construction of the Meldrum Tunnel, and several were discovered by the Idarado. However there is still a lot of unexplored territory in the potentially rich areas along the proposed tunnel's path.

The project had to be abandoned in 1900 for lack of financing. Only 2.2 miles of the six mile project was complete. Meldrum died a pauper; ironically he was the one who was grubstaking Robinson and his prospecting partners when they discovered the Yankee Girl Mine eighteen years earlier.

OURAY FREIGHTING
A Very Big Business

⚜ ⚜

Freighting in and out of Ouray was big business in the early days of the town. Freighting in the San Juan Mountains started out with burros and burro punchers, as there was nothing but Indian trails to follow through the mountains. Mules needed a fairly good trail. A well-used Ute trail could possibly be used by mules but it would be necessary to go where the Utes were going or a burro trail could be upgraded into a mule trail. The county and state had no money to do road work (and it was not common for them to do so anywhere in the United States at the time), so the job of road building was usually left to the freighter. If he did anything at all, it was usually to get the biggest rocks or stumps out of the "road" or throw a few logs over a creek to form a "bridge." Eventually true wagon roads were constructed, but most of these early roads were toll roads and the freighter had to pay to get the freight across them.

Often even the toll roads were still very crude and the bigger freighters had to have large numbers of men ready to repair the roads and their wagons, and veterinarians were often hired on a full time basis to take care of their animals. Large stables and barns were needed to protect the animals, especially in the winter, and warehouses were used to store the animal's food, which often had to be freighted in, especially during the winter. When teams were used, there were harnesses to make and fix, blacksmiths to make repairs and shoe the animals (they used special cleated horseshoes in the winter), and ranchers needed to supply hay and grains. The horses that were used to pull freight wagons were usually huge Percherons and Clydesdales, with six to a team and with up to twelve pulling the really big loads like steam boilers for the mines. However long, thin, but heavy loads like mine rail, pipes, and lumber were still normally tied to the sides of mules or burros and drug to the mines. Lumber was usually cut a little longer than needed as some of its length would be gone after the trip. A large freighting company might therefore easily employ several hundred men in its operation. Some have estimated that there were more men involved directly or indirectly in the freight business than there were miners and prospectors in the San Juan Mountains.

A burro could carry 150 to 200 pounds, a mule about 250, and a wagon a ton or two of rough, hard ore, so the wagons and especially their wheels and axles had to be extremely hardy. This meant that the empty wagon itself was heavier and more costly than a normal wagon. It took six or more horses or mules to pull freight in the mountains, so the weight per animal was only a little above 350 pounds. All of this cost money (the going shipping rate was two to three cents a pound by wagon) so freight rates were very expensive, making it economical to only ship the richest ores. Some freighters made more money than the mines whose ore they were shipping.

Freighters (probably from John Ashenfelter's operation) line up to take Camp Bird concentrates to the train in Ouray for shipment.

(Author's Collection)

It was about 300 miles from Ouray to an efficient smelter – all of it over some of the roughest country Colorado had to offer. Worse yet to some of these rough and rugged men in Ouray, was that those taking their wagons through the Ute reservation were not allowed to have whiskey with them, and some of these routes could take two weeks or more! There was also the human freight – an average of 200 passengers a day in the San Juans, translating into several dozen runs. As soon as there was a wagon road, some huge and heavy machinery for the mines was sent to the San Juan mines and mills. Initially oxen were used to pull these loads, usually six or eight to a wagon, but they were slow and not used much after the 1880s. If you wonder what distinguished oxen from a cow, there is no difference except their use. Oxen were merely bulls bred to be big and muscular not "beefy." If not using oxen, some freighters resorted to using ten and twelve horse teams to pull the big loads, and when quantity not weight was the issue these ten and twelve horse teams might pull as many as three wagons hitched together. The driver of these teams was called a "teamster," and they were the best paid men in the entire freighting operation.

Freighting to Ouray before the arrival of the railroad was big business. Not only for freight coming to the town, but for the freighting of food, mining equipment and supplies to the nearby mines and mining camps. Much of the need for freight coming to Ouray by wagon was eliminated by the railroad but the freighting out of Ouray continues to this day in small part by trucks.

Ouray's and the San Juan's largest and best regarded freight company was that of Dave Wood, who came to Colorado in 1876 and started his business in Del Norte. As new discoveries were made and new settlements built, Wood grew his business into the mountains to the west. Where there was no town he would help build one, his livery stables and warehouses for freight usually being the largest structure in the town. Dave got his freight through no matter what the weather, changing out wheels for skids when the snow was too deep. He also took passengers, and it wasn't long before his freight operation was the biggest in all of Colorado. When a lady asked him how long he had lived in the San Juans, he answered, "Madam, I hauled these mountains in here." The woman supposedly replied, "Oh, then you must be Dave Wood." Dave became a very wealthy man. However he invested much of his earnings back into the mines he was serving. In doing so, he lost virtually everything in the Silver Crash of 1893.

John Ashenfelter was the largest and best of the local Ouray freighters. At one time he was said to have thirty-two freight wagons with six horse teams, over one hundred burros and mules that were used when there was no wagon road to his destination, and over fifty saddle horses which were rented by people going into the mountains who would often let them go when they got to their destination and the horses would come straight back to their Ouray stable on their own.

Although Wood and his family originally lived all over the San Juans (much of the time in Lake City or Gunnison), his family moved to Ouray in 1885. He brought with him his sister's husband James W. Abbott to manage the local operation and Dave bought a ranch just outside today's Ridgway. The record keeping of the many freight transfers was mind-boggling and the value of each sack of ore could be radically different. The same thing occurred when supplies came in by wagon that were reloaded onto pack trains. Coordination was also needed to try to keep the wagons going up with supplies, coming back with ore. Even when the D&RG Railroad came to Ouray the freighters were still needed to get the freight up to the mining camps and get the ore down from the mines in the railroad. So although the freight business decreased a bit, it lasted until well into the twentieth century.

A large burro train (probably Ashenfelter's) loaded with ore from the Revenue Mine that will go to the railroad in Ouray.

(Author's Collection)

Prospectors, Miners, and Mining

THE DISCOVERY OF THE YANKEE GIRL MINE
The Mine That Made Ouray

⁓ ⁓

The Yankee Girl Mine was discovered on August 14, 1882 by John Robinson. It was the mine that would draw enormous attention to the Red Mountain Mining District, which was located half way between Silverton and Ouray. That in turn helped bring attention to San Juan mines as a whole, and mining boomed. John Robinson was working at the Guston Mine, basically looking for lead to use as flux in the local smelters. He was mainly a prospector, but he and his three prospecting partners needed money for more supplies. On this day however, he was deer hunting, and while resting he saw an interesting rock. When he picked it up to examine it, he realized it was much too heavy for its size – a sure sign it contained metals. When he broke it open he could see it was solid galena – a silver and lead ore.

Within days from the discovery Robinson and his three partners, who had agreed to share in anyone's discovery, were shipping 4,500 pounds of ore by burro train to Ouray every day and it was averaging eighty-eight ounces of silver and 56% lead per ton. One month after its discovery the Yankee Girl was sold for $125,000. In its first year of production the Yankee Girl shipped $450,000 in silver-lead galena, and the ore was getting richer with depth, which might or might not happen in the San Juans. There are widely fluctuating estimates of how much the Yankee Girl produced before it shut down in the mid-1890s (not for lack of ore but rather because of water flooding their workings). The mine had reached a depth of 1,050 feet. Ore for the first seventy-five feet averaged seventy ounces of silver. The next eighty feet averaged 242 ounces of silver. At a depth of 300 to 400 feet some of its ore averaged over 1,000 ounces of silver per ton, but after that its ore quickly decreased in value with depth and it was expensive to use its huge copper-lined pumps, which was so lined because water was producing sulfuric acid in the shafts.

The Yankee Girl's shaft house still stands on Red Mountain and is very visible from the road. It is a favorite subject for today's photographers, but almost every other remnant is gone.   (Author's Collection)

The Meldrum Tunnel (previously discussed) was one project to lower costs and the Joker Tunnel was an attempt to strike the ore of several of Red Mountain's best mines at a lower lever and economically drain water from many of the Red Mountain mines. The main mines to be worked by the tunnel were the Genesee-Vanderbilt, Guston, and the Yankee Girl. These had all been rich mines that were following large "chimney deposits" straight down into the earth. The Joker was only a tunnel and not a mine and was located about a mile south of Ironton along side the Silverton Railroad, but ordinary ore cars brought the ore from the tunnel to the surface. The tunnel was driven in the early 1900s and financed in great part by the then owner of the Silverton Railroad, who hoped to get their line operating again as well as getting part of the profits from the tunnel. Mining operations were actually commenced after several of the first deposits were reached, but the ore was low grade and the tunnel was stopped at about 4,600 feet in length before it reached the mines that had been the richest in the area. Later on during and shortly after the Great Depression, the Joker was again worked by a very small crew at a profit, but was abandoned by World War II.

THE MINERAL FARM
But You Couldn't Eat Its Products

⌇⌇⌇ ⌇⌇⌇

The Mineral Farm was discovered a few months after the discovery of the Ouray bowl by John Eckles and A. W. "Gus" Begole in July of 1875. Eckles and Begole recognized that there were valuable veins in the Ouray bowl and went back to Baker's Park for enough supplies to allow them to spend the summer, but word got out of their new discovery and soon other prospectors were showing up. Soon A. J. Staley and Logan Whitlock filed on the Trout and the Fisherman Lodes (they had been fishing near Box Canyon at the time of their discoveries). Begole, Jacob Ohlwiler and John Morrow filed the Cedar and the Clipper Mining Claims on August 1875. All of these mineral discoveries were made in or very near the future City of Ouray city limits and the prospectors soon formed the Uncompahgre Mining District and a townsite they called "Uncompahgre." The Trout and Fisherman lodes were the first to mine and shipped ore before winter set in by way of the Uncompahgre Valley and the Ute Indian Reservation. Cline and Long even started placing stakes in the heavily wooded bowl to show the location of future streets and alleys (there was as much money from selling lots as most men made from prospecting.)

In October of 1875 Begole and Eckles filed the Mineral Farm Lode, named for the minerals on the claim being as easy to harvest as vegetables from a garden. Begole and Eckels worked the mine for several years but did not have the capital to fully develop the mine; and, as did many prospectors, sold it in the fall of 1878 for $150,000 – the equivalent of several million dollars today.

The mine was noted as only .8 miles from Ouray as the crow flies, but perhaps double or triple that distance with elevation gain and the roundabout trip of getting there. The *Ouray Times* of December 14, 1878, excitedly reported:

> *The transfer makes an epic in the history of mining in this section
> and ushers in the dawn of prosperity for our people and town...
> Business will undoubtedly be better and money more plentiful this
> winter that ever before...*

Begole demanded and received his half in cash on the spot. The
Ouray Times wrote:

> *The new owners invested heavily in new workings and a mill and
> did well. The mine eventually produced over a million dollars. A
> few placer claims were also filed on the Uncompahgre in October
> 1875 after the Mineral Farm's location, but before winter set in. A
> few prospectors spent the winter of 1875-76 in the Ouray area so
> as to be the first to make claims in the spring.*

*After selling the Mineral Farm Mine A. W. Begole moved to Ouray and
opened one of its first stores. Gordon Kimball was another early arrival.*

(Author's Collection)

The Mineral Farm operated for many more years but Begole and Eckles were the only ones to make a substantial profit from the operation because of the expenses involved with mining, transporting, and smelting the ore. A variety of minerals were mined there including gold, silver, ankerite, barite, copper, and chalcopyrite. In the 1930s the mine was still operating and employed thirty to forty workers at the mine or its mill. Later in the 1960s to 1990s the mine was famous to mineral collectors for the mineral (especially quartz) crystals that were taken from its veins.

Begole took his cash money and opened a store in Ouray which did well. Later he moved to his ranch near Delta. Unfortunately he then went back to mining and died dead broke.

The Mineral Farm was at its biggest about 1930. This was the mine's mill and offices.

(Author's Collection)

THE SILVER CAVE
All the World's Jewels Were Stored Here By Nature

❧ ❧

The National Belle Mine, located inside the limits of Red Mountain City, was one of the San Juans' most famous mines. Much of its ore, although not extremely rich, was so soft that it was merely shoveled into sacks, loaded just outside the shaft house into gondola cars on the Silverton Railroad, and shipped to the smelter. The costs of mining could not have been lower. Although it produced over a $9 million, it was most famous for its silver cave that was so amazing that the mine's owners took the unheard of step of stopping mining operations for some time so that the general public could come and see what had been discovered for themselves. Ernest Ingersoll in his book *Crest of the Continent* gives us the description of what the miners first saw (he also wrote a novel based on the discovery of the Silver Cave:

> *A workman broke through the walls (of a tunnel) into a cave. Hollow echoes came back from the blows of his pick, and stones thrown were heard to roll a long distance. Taking a candle, one of the men descended and found himself in an immense chamber, the flickering rays of the light showing him the vaulted roof far above, seamed with bright streaks of galena (a silver-lead ore) and interspersed with masses of soft carbonates, chlorides, and pure white talc. On different sides of this remarkable chamber were small openings leading to other rooms or chambers, showing the same rich formation. Returning from this brief reconnaissance, the party began regular exploration. They crept through the opening into an immense natural tunnel running above and across the route of their working drift for a hundred feet or more, over which they clamored over great bowlders (sic) of pure galena, and mounds of soft grey carbonates, while the walls and roof showed themselves a solid mass of carbonate ores of silver. Returning to the starting*

point they passed through another narrow tunnel of solid and glittering galena for a distance of forty feet, and found indications of other large passages and chambers beyond… It would seem as though Nature had gathered her choice treasures from her inexhaustible storehouse, and wrought these tunnels, natural stoping places (caves) and chambers, studded with glittering crystals and bright minerals to dazzle the eyes of man in after ages, and lure him on to other treasures hidden deeper in the bowels of the earth.

The Red Mountain Pilot (July 21, 1883) wrote:

The National Belle Mine and its "Silver Cave" was right in the middle of Red Mountain Town and next to the Silverton Railroad. Travel writer Ernest Ingersol was so enchanted with the cave that he wrote a novel about it.

(Author's Collection)

No where(sic) else in the world is there such a large body of mineral as there is at the National Belle and no one knows the extent of the mineral. There is a million tons in sight and no one can estimate the value… One of the best features about the rich discovery is that the present owners were the original locaters and they will reap the fruit of their toil instead of some tin head capitalist.

The prospectors who discovered the mine did not have the money to develop it but sold the mine for $160,000 (again millions of dollars in today's values). The ore averaged about $75 per ton, but operating costs were so low that initially about half of that amount was profit.

GOLD MINING IN OURAY DURING THE GREAT DEPRESSION
They Made a Good Living

The Great Depression played huge economic havoc over most of the United States, but one place that was somewhat spared was Colorado, and in particular most of its mining towns, including Ouray. One author, David Lavender in his book *One Man's West* gives us a peek at life at the mines when he hired on with the Camp Bird in 1933. Just to have a job was good, but he needed to get money to get married and earned five dollars a day there instead of the thirty dollars a month he had earned previously as a cowboy or the three to four dollars a day of average wage earners at that time. Lavender wrote why the mines were open and paying so well at such a desperate time.

> *The mines had finished working the best ore bodies about the time that labor and material costs began an upward spiral during the early decades of the century. They could not raise the retail cost of their commodity for the value of gold was fixed by law. So the mines languished as gold mines do during times of prosperity. Then along came the depression of the '30s. Down went production costs again. Meanwhile more efficient methods of ore production had been developed, and it was possible to work ground the earlier companies had ignored.... President Roosevelt suddenly had pegged the price of gold from $20.67 per ounce to eventually nearly $36... The rush to the hills took on almost the color of a stampede. A pale color, however.*

Even though he was making very good money, Lavender chose to quit the Camp Bird Mine in September of 1933. The winter isolation and the dangers of avalanches and the work were just too much for him, but there were other men ready to take his job.

Gold prices had also risen in Europe. For a while, American citizens could buy or mine gold in the United States and sell it in Europe at a profit. The value of the dollar was decreasing; so another reason to get gold was its value was staying pretty much the same. Cripple Creek, Alma, the San Juans, and other gold bearing areas in Colorado opened up again. It wasn't a boom, but mining was profitable if the ore was rich enough. Even though the gold being mined was usually so small that the miner could not even see it, some of the Depression gold miners asked to be paid in gold.

Yet another form of gold rush occurred for individuals, many of whom only learned how to pan gold from the WPA. Whole families were camped along rivers and creeks known to still have some gold. Individuals and some companies also reworked the tailings of gold mills known to have been inefficient, and did so at a profit. All of these people did fairly well until World War II when the government no longer allowed gold to be processed in favor of mining heavy metals like copper, lead and zinc which were needed for the war effort. However mining continued in the San Juans as most local mines had base metals to sell for the war. If a little gold showed up with the base metals, so the better.

Prospectors panning for gold have just found some good size nuggets.
(Author's Collection)

TWO LOST GOLD VEINS
Do Hikers Pass One Every Day?

Most lost gold mine tales take place high up in the mountains, but Ouray has several places close to town where one might look for a rich gold vein. One is supposed to be along Oak Creek, somewhere up on Twin Peaks, but along the creek and not the hiking trail. Prospectors who came while the area was still Ute territory supposedly found the rich vein in or very near Oak Creek, but could do no mining because there were constantly Ute Indians in the Ouray bowl. They left when their supplies ran out and came back later, but could not find the rich vein. Their problem in great part is that there are many small waterfalls coming over high ledges in the creek, making it impossible to hike directly up the creek. However if the trail up Twin Peaks is near the creek you might take a peek.

The other lost vein is probably somewhere along Bear Creek Trail, just a few miles out of town. Much more effort has been spent searching for what is usually called "The Lost Swede Mine," but is actually a vein. Sometimes the lost vein is called "The Crazy Swede Mine," as it is said by some that the man who made the discovery (a Swede) went crazy trying to find the spot again. The lost Swede was traveling in the early 1900s during the dead of winter. He had been working at the Golden Fleece Mine, which was only about three miles from Lake City, but he wanted to spend the winter in Ouray. He hiked up the Engineer Pass Road to Roses' Cabin and was crossing American Flats to the headwaters of the Bear Creek Trail when a terrible snowstorm hit. He eventually thought he had struck the trail and started down the mountain. When the storm worsened even more, the Swede looked for shelter and on the opposite side of the creek from the trail the Swede found a small crevice in a rock cliff that he squeezed into. As he wiggled further into the crevice he discovered a seam of quartz that ran perpendicular into the ground in front of him and at the back of the

Bear Creek Trail is rough, steep, and narrow, even though the county at one time claimed it as a road. There were plenty of places for a rich vein of gold to hide.
(Author's Collection)

crevice. The seam was filled with gold – lots of it! He broke off pieces of the quartz and gold-filled rock and put it in two pairs of extra socks he had with him. After the storm ended he went on, half frozen, to Ouray. In the process of warming the Swede up, his sample rocks were seen by others and everyone was amazed at their richness in gold. The ore in his socks was assayed and was sold for a very good price – enough to keep the Swede in wine, women, and song for the rest of the winter.

Some said the Swede had obviously just high-graded (stolen the ore while a miner at the Golden Fleece Mine) and used the "lost mine" story as a legal explanation to allow his rich stash of gold to be sold without being arrested or even suspected. There was super-rich ore in places in the Golden Wonder Mine, and some spectators said it looked like it could have come from that mine. However, once his money was gone the Swede tried to relocate the mine. He went back to the headwaters of Bear Creek in American Flats but wasn't even sure which canyon he had gone down from there. He searched off and on for years, and found several likely crevices, but no vein. Avalanches or rock slides may have covered the vein, and perhaps someday it will be uncovered again. Many people in Lake City think the Sweede had started down the Cow Creek drainage that also begins in American Flats. This is possible, but people have also searched there. The whole upper Cow Creek area is a place where many people beside the Sweede have become lost. Be very careful if you go there.

THE AMERICAN NETTIE MINE
Hanging By a Thread

The American Nettie was a rich but somewhat limited and spotty gold mine, but it and the Camp Bird Mines were two of the operations that helped the people of Ouray keep working after the Silver Panic of 1893. Both had lead, zinc, copper and silver; but it was the gold that kept the mines operating. The American Nettie was only 8/10ths of a mile as the crow flies from Ouray and could be seen from some parts of town.

Before the discovery of the American Nettie, there was some gold found in the cliffs immediately to the northeast of town. The "Blowout" was an area of obvious mineral penetration, but no one seemed to be able to find much gold there. Later, some geologists speculated that there was substantial gold that was pushed out of a very large and rich vein that millions of years ago stretched between Twin Peaks and the Blowout but which was totally washed away when the local giant glaciers were melting and the river was much larger than today. Placer gold was found eleven miles downstream in the Uncompahgre River in an area between Ridgway and the Ridgway Reservoir. Several million in gold were mined from the American Nettie, but the original vein could have contained many more millions.

However the American Nettie is probably, of all things, most famous for its outhouse. The mine's boarding house was built on at the top of a ledge hundreds of feet in the air; and the outhouse for the boarding house was built so that it hung out over the edge of the ledge. When being used, the occupant hung out into space in a structure that didn't look like it was all that stable. There was only one outhouse for the men, women, and children who were at the mine, but it was said by some of its occupants that "no one lingered in it for long." To make matters worse the hole for the outhouse sometimes clogged with blowing snow and ice in the winter, and it was then necessary

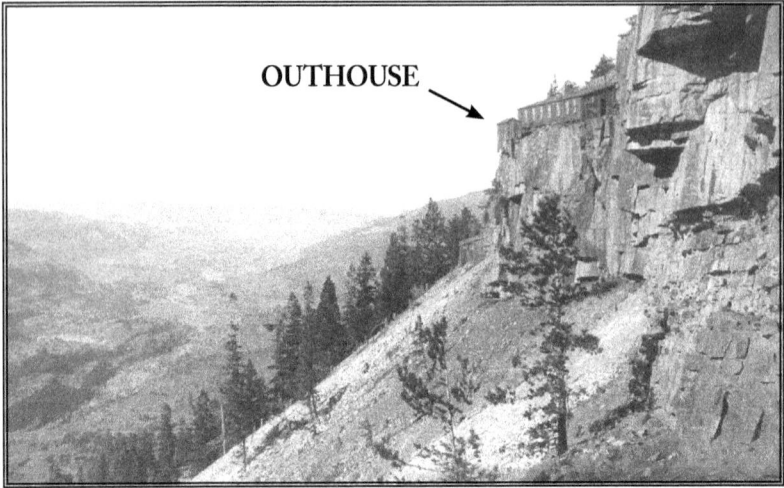

The American Nettie can be seen from Ouray, yet it was high above. The large area south of the mine is "The Blowout" formed by highly mineralized solutions from deep within the earth. It did not contain much gold or silver, however, so it hasn't been mined – yet.

(Author's Collection)

to beat on that frozen mass to open it up – all while standing in the flimsy structure. It is worthy to note that no one ever got hurt in the outhouse, although there may have been some that had an accident.

Whether traveling on horseback or on foot it was a very long, hard walk from Ouray to get to the American Nettie Mine, and a long way to get its ore down, so someone finally came up with the idea of putting in an aerial tram from the mine down to the valley floor alongside the river at a point nearly opposite where Rotary Park is today, but on the other side of the Uncompahgre River. This greatly reduced time and effort and the mine even built a power plant along the river at the same point and ran electricity up to it along the tram cables. Miners would then usually ride up to the mine in the tram.

The tram crossing the valley stood as a landmark for a long time until a low-flying pilot ran into it and crashed. All the remains of the operation were then taken down.

PROSPECTORS AND MINERS
There is a Big Differences

Most people use the words "prospector" and "miner" interchangeably, but there is a big difference between the two occupations, and they were very different types of men. The prospector reported to no one but himself, except a few did have a wife. The prospector was "footloose and fancy free," going where he wanted and when he wanted. His only worldly possessions were usually his mining tools, his burro, and a dog or two. He would often be away from civilization for six months or more and usually did not have a house or a log cabin, and many disdained even a tent. They usually ate under a tree and had the same food every day – pork belly (bacon), coffee, beans, every now and then a canned good (like syrup, corn, tomatoes, or peaches from their meager supply, and flour for pancakes). Although he might have a sheltered spot or occasionally own a tent, he usually slept outside on the ground. If he did have a cabin it was low, only a few logs high, and with sod for a roof could be constructed in only a few days. He was not usually hunting for precious minerals for the money; much more often it was simply for the excitement or the adventure. Most prospectors sold their mineral discoveries as soon as they found them and usually for relatively inexpensive amounts. Then they went to look for a new discovery. Prospectors did not generally believe in geologists as they knew that gold was "simply where you found it." They did however soon have a few simple rules for prospecting, such as veins were usually richer the higher up they were found, but where they might be found was very unpredictable; and a vein might be only a fraction of an inch in one place and close by be feet across, so it paid to follow a small rich vein for a while. A vein might run for many miles or be only a few feet long, so it paid to try to follow a vein.

A miner, as opposed to a prospector, was usually an hourly wage worker; although sometimes they had contracts to do a certain amount of work for a certain amount of money. The miner wanted a regular job, with regular hours, and the knowledge that he always knew where the next meal was coming from. If he was single that meal usually came from a cook in the mine's boarding house for which he paid room and board. The food was usually good as the cooks were 'fueling" the mine's work engine. Married men often had a place to live at the mine, or they might build a little shanty nearby for themselves and their family. Miners were usually looking for certainty in their life, while prospectors lived day by day. Miners lived by the clock (usually a mine whistle) and by the rules, while prospectors didn't need a watch and had very few rules. Miners had very few decisions to make – they just followed the rules and orders of their boss man. The prospector was trying to find where he would get rich.

Prospectors were often grubstaked by others in order to do their work. Miners were sometimes allowed to run a tab. Many early San Juan prospectors threw away gold ore thinking it was worthless. If you think that is bad remember there was an entire generation of

A mine owner has decided to start mining and his burros carry powder, rail, and a large blacksmith's bellow, among other equipment and supplies. The Bucket of Blood Saloon is to the left across the street.

(Author's Collection)

prospectors that that the Leadville black sand was worthless when in fact it was rich silver. They were looking for gold nuggets such as were found in California. Finally they learned that the soft, dull-gray, worthless looking rock or sand they threw away was often silver, lead, and copper, sometimes combined with Tellurium gold. No matter how rich your vein was, there were other factors that needed to be determined before you could consider yourself a rich man. As in real estate matters, location, location, location was important. Was there a safe spot nearby to tunnel into the mountain? Was there water nearby for a mill or at least for the drills? Was there a road nearby, and if not, how much would it cost to build one? Was your ore of a variety that assayers and chemists had already determined how to easily and inexpensively get the minerals out? These and other matters were important because if it cost more to get your ore to a smelter, then you had nothing but a money pit. Many early San Juan mining investors learned this rule the hard way.

Two totally unprepared and unexperienced prospectors with only a pick and shovel and no supplies. They are doomed to fail and perhaps die!
(Author's Collection)

How Did Tom Walsh Discover the Camp Bird Mine?
It's Not An Easy Answer?

〜 〜

Tom Walsh was not a typical prospector. Actually he was not really even a prospector, but rather a mill operator and assayer. Walsh was, however, one of the most experienced mining men in the San Juans – in fact he had a degree in mineralogy. He had bought and sold mines all over Colorado and operated mining mills in several different places, but rarely, if at all, was he the prospector who actually discovered the vein. Tom Walsh, founder of the fabulously rich Camp Bird Mine in 1896, knew what he was doing – using other men's hardships and discoveries to hopefully make himself rich. For years he examined prospects, bought and sold mines, and "almost made it." For this and other reasons it is not even correct to say that "Walsh discovered the Camp Bird Mine."

In 1894 he had moved to Silverton where he ran a smelter. He had bought mines near Silverton and Rico, but a condensed story of the "Camp Bird discovery," as his daughter, Evalyn Walsh McClean later wrote it in her book *Father Struck It Rich* is as follows:

> *Father himself was far from well and spent much of his energy in sleepless nights. A whole series of ventures had gone wrong through no fault of his. A drop in the price of silver had turned a profitable smelter at Kokomo into a liability.... These and other investments had become unprofitable or else had been mortgaged or sold to provide him with funds to engage in some further mining enterprises. The depression of 1893 had contributed to his worries....*

Evalyn said Walsh wrote at this time to a friend:

> *I am very poor. I have nothing to look forward to.... I gave checks amounting to $675... (and) when my other checks out come in there will be only $50 to meet this $675.*

Evalyn continued:

Tom Walsh never was a prospector or miner. He was an assayer and a mill and smelter operator and owner which allowed him to find new discoveries from the people that came to his businesses.

(Author's Collection)

Father did hold on some-how. His imagination was bewitched. He felt there were richer depos-its of minerals in the earth than had ever been found.... In Imogene Basin, nine miles from Ouray, was an area that particularly held his interest.... Along in the eighties millions of dollars had been expended there in developing silver-lead veins and in the erection of mills.... He wanted copper.... If he could find a copper mine or an iron mine or both, he could bring success to the pyritic smelter he was trying to develop in Ouray.... As he talked I could almost hear the racket of hoisting machinery, the grinding pulsations of big concentrating plants; yes, even the clink of shovels and picks of the men who once had dug inside the hills that threw their cool shadows over us as we rested.... "They were looking for silver," he said and squatted on top of a rockslide –"In the mining game gold is just where you happen to find it. And you never know what is under your feet."

Tom Walsh had to be bed-ridden with a case of jaundice after this trip into Imogene Basin with his daughter; but he called for his friend Andy Richardson to go back and remove the snow from the tunnel entrance where they had been. Andy took samples from the tunnel and Walsh had them assayed. Walsh was again bedridden after being up

for a few days, so when they were alone in the house he called Evalyn
to his bed and asked if she remembered the time they had spent in
Imogene Basin. Evalyn continues:

> He motioned me to come around to the side of the bed and showed
> me a piece of grayish quartz. It was not very impressive. He wet
> it with his tongue and held it near my eyes. Like thread-ends in
> its texture were glistening circles and specks of black. "That's gold,"
> he said.... The report that he had received on the sample was better
> than his wildest dreams.

Evalyn wondered why he was telling her – a young girl – about the
discovery, but he whispered, "daughter I have struck it rich!" Even if
he died from his illness, someone in the family would now live to tell
others the secret. But he did live. The sample he had shown Evalyn
showed over a thousand ounces of gold per ton of waste rock. The
development of the mine paid for the equipment needed and allowed
him to build what Evalyn called "the great gold engine."

> The great gold engine my father had brought into existence high up
> in the mountains was making its loudest grinding clamor as we
> returned to it.... The sounds were the echoes of instruments that
> had been shaped first in his mind and only after that conception
> had received a synthesis in what could be called a reality.... The
> Camp Bird was producing $5,000 a day (about $100,000 today).
> Each morning we Walshes arose richer than we had gone to bed.
> Mine and mill ran day and night.

There are many other stories of how Walsh "discovered the Camp
Bird," and Walsh himself gave different accounts depending on the
occasion. Years later when he gave the commencement address at
Colorado School of Mines he recounted a very scientific approach.
Walsh said that Andy Richardson indicated he knew there was gold
in Imogene Basin, just not how much. Some others also say Walsh
came to Imogene at the request of Andy Richardson, who said there
was lots of gold there. Evalyn writes that her father was looking for
flux for his smelter, but Walsh said he had seen signs of gold in ore
brought to his smelter in Silverton from mines in Imogene Basin.
Walsh on another occasion said he only recognized the signs of gold
when in Imogene Basin, but had Andy sample some of the dumps

to see if an assay would actually show gold. At any rate, the rich tellurium gold in Imogene Basin had been either bypassed or not recognized until Tom Walsh came to look himself and recognized that the region needed to be carefully checked out and assayed for gold. Many say that his discovery was the biggest, richest gold mine ever owned by a single individual.

Evelyn's story of her later "jinxed" life is told in more detail in another part of this book. As opposed to his daughter, Walsh is remembered in Ouray as a very generous, if not humble, man. He donated money to townspeople to pay off their mortgage when they were down and out. He helped the Sisters of Mercy Hospital in Ouray by paying off their mortgage allowing them to stay afloat until they were supported by the local mines, he contributed to all the churches in Ouray regardless of denomination, until the time of his death, and he did much, much more. He donated the money to build a second floor on the Ouray City Hall and furnished it with one of the largest and most expensive libraries on the Western Slope of Colorado. Walsh remained a generous man until the time of his death, but he knew his family might blow his fortune, which they mostly did even though he put much of his wealth into trusts that he thought would preserve his fortune over many years. Evalyn died penniless.

The Camp Bird Mill and buildings was a mile or two downhill from the mine. By the size of the tailings pond it is about 1930.

(Author's Collection)

This photo is very unusual for miners thought it bad luck for women to be underground at the time. Note they are using candles for light.
(Author's Collection)

Miners about 1920 drilling upwards with pneumatic drills. Different bits for the drill and a geologist checking ore are also shown.
(Author' Collection)

Ghosts, Ghost Towns & Legends

GHOSTS TOWNS IN
OURAY COUNTY
There Are Many of Them

⁓ ⁓

Ouray County was filled with small settlements that are now ghosts towns or which now do not exist at all. Since San Miguel County was a part of Ouray County until six years after Ouray County was originally formed, some of these settlements may now be in San Miguel County. The ghost towns include Ash, Aurora, Campbird, Dallasville, Gabbert, Guston, Ironton, Lawrence, Mount Sneffles (or simply Sneffles), Portland, Rogersville, Ruby City, Virginius, Wareville, and Windham. These sites all had post offices, although the Rogersville post office existed for less than three months, Ruby City for fourteen months, and Wareville only two months. This just shows how easily a post office could be obtained in those days.

Some of the locations of these "towns" are not known. Some say Aurora was about four miles west of Ridgway near the junction of the East and West Forks of Dallas Creek, but other sources say it was later known as and was on or near "Dallas Divide." It would be assumed that Dallasville was just another name for Dallas near today's Ridgway Reservoir, but post office records show they were two different spots. There was also a spot called Dallas Fork in this area. Gabbert was a spot on the D&RG immediately north of the junction of Cow Creek and the Uncompahgre River. This would put it just downstream from the Ridgway Dam of today. Lawrence was around the old Dave Wood ranch and was soon moved north to Dallas. Rogersville was very close to Red Mountain Town and was one of the first towns in the Red Mountain Mining District. Ruby City was on upper Cow Creek but its only record is that it appears on a few maps at a spot where some still later maps showed a few cabins. Wareville's location is not even generally known. It only appears in the post office records and perhaps was just someone's house. Lawrence was moved to Dallas. Mt. Sneffels changed to just Sneffels. Windham was at the very south end of the

Uncomphgre Valley where a mill was established. It was definitely a "company town," if a town at all. Plummer had a post office in 1900 to 1901, and was not moved, but where was it?

Then there are towns that neither appear on maps or had a post office. In the Red Mountain District were Joker (probably near or at the Joker Tunnel), Congress, Red Mountain City (above the Congress Mine), Copper Glen (perhaps an original name for Ironton, Sweetville perhaps originally what was later called Chattanoga (in San Juan County), Hudson (probably at the Hudson Mine), Missouri City (somewhere near the Yankee Boy Mine), Del Mino (which was accessed through Silverton via Mineral Creek), and Hot Springs (probably at Orvis hot springs pool, but before the Utes moved away). There was also a town called Park City that was noted by the Hayden Survey in 1873 in Ironton Park, but which this author has never seen any other mention.

There are undoubtedly other small settlements that have been overlooked here, but this gives you just some idea of the confusion of trying to go to towns then or now, when no one knew where they were located. Only Ouray, Ridgway, and Colona now exist as towns in Ouray County.

The ghost town of Joker near the Joker Tunnel only has one building still standing (so it is hard to tell it is a "ghost town"), but is right next to the Million Dollar Highway.   (Author's Collection)

GHOSTS IN THE CITY OF OURAY
The Old Hospital Is a Likely Spot

Like many old western mining towns, Ouray has its set of ghost stories; a few of the most famous being mentioned here – the ghost(s) in Ouray's Sisters of Mercy Hospital (now the Ouray County Historical Society's museum), the Beaumont Hotel, and the Western Hotel.

What is now Ouray's very fine museum was originally a hospital, built for its people, and especially the miners of Ouray, and owned and run by the Catholic Church and the Order of the Sisters of Mercy. Ouray's residents, and especially the miners, were in dire need of such a facility because of the many dangers in the area – accidents at the mines, pneumonia, avalanches, wild beasts, and many other events that could easily hurt or kill a person. The hospital included an operating room, a maternity ward, and single and double rooms for the patients. The nuns lived in the basement where they also cooked and did laundry for the hospital and ran a decently stocked pharmacy. Local miners paid a fee of one dollar a month to be eligible for their services, if needed.

The hospital eventually closed and the building sat empty for many years but was still owned by the Catholic Church next door. In the 1970s the hospital was sold at a low price to the local historical society, which kept some of the more special rooms "as is" and started converting others into displays of various sorts for a county museum. The author was given permission to modify the part of the basement used to iron sheets into a mining tunnel to display the museum's many mining treasures. Late one stormy winter night when he was working in the basement alone, he heard the first floor's front door open and close and someone walk down the central hallway to the basement stairs at the back of the building. This was a little unusual as only four or five people had keys to the museum and he thought the door was locked.

Quickly going upstairs, it was discovered that no one was there. The entire museum was carefully checked on the chance that the steps

St. Joseph Miner's Hospital was built in 1887 and was the scene of many deaths. Now the Ouray County Historical Museum, it is the perfect hangout for ghosts. (Author's Collection)

might have come from an intruder and that perhaps the front door was left unlocked. The door was locked, and when he stepped outside the author discovered that it had been snowing heavily and there were no footprints in the snow or down the hall. So as not to be thought crazy the author kept quiet about the event. Almost exactly a year later, another member of the society's board was in the basement stoking the coal-burning heater located there when exactly the same event occurred, but this time the society's member talked of the situation with others. No logical reason for getting in the front locked door, footsteps all the way down the long hall, or the lack of footsteps in fresh snow or snow along the hall were ever found. Since that time other ghosts have been reported. What a wonderful place to hear ghosts and learn the real history about the area.

THE BEAUMONT GHOSTS
Still Interested in the Real World

The Beaumont Hotel supposedly has several regular ghosts. One is a woman ghost who is said to walk throughout the hotel's halls at 2:15 a.m. on the night of each quarter moon (the anniversary of her death). It is said that her husband murdered her in the hotel and she is looking for him for revenge. She stops at various doors and rattles the door knobs as if she needs to turn the knob to get in.

Another Beaumont ghost is a woman who was a maid at the Beaumont, who lived in the maid's quarters on the third story of the hotel. She was shot four times by the hotel's jealous pastry chef, who was immediately jailed and angry townspeople burned the jail down and killed him the very night of the maid's murder. The young woman's ghost has been seen from outside the hotel pulling back curtains at various spots and looking out windows on various nights beginning shortly after her death, and she is occasionally seen crying inside the hotel.

It is said that the people who made the early sightings recognized who the ghost was, but since over a century had passed since the murder, no one still recognizes the woman, but some guests have taken photos of hazy objects that could be ghosts in the Beaumont.

Owners and managers of the hotel over the years have almost all said the whole hotel seems haunted but that the spirits are friendly. They also report paranormal activity like rattling door knobs, colored lights, and strange noises.

THE WESTERN HOTEL GHOSTS
More Recent Sightings

~~ ~~

One interesting fact in all the ghost stories told here is that the buildings were all vacant for long periods of years over time, and perhaps the ghosts felt the buildings to be places they would be undisturbed, although all the buildings were eventually restored and put back into use and a few ghosts were seen in all three places before they stood empty for long periods.

The Western Hotel is one of largest all wooden hotels remaining in the West. Several specific rooms are supposed to be haunted, and many one-time quick sightings have been made. One very logical spot in the hotel would be in the full basement, but guests and employees are not often down there. The author was an Ouray realtor at one time and had the hotel listed for sale. On more than one occasion prospective buyers wanted to tour the hotel, including the basement so as to check out the foundation. Although it was a full basement it was divided into several rooms. In later years one part of the basement was used by Tuffy Flor, Ouray's undertaker, to prepare bodies for burial. Many of his tools, including a bloodletting table and a rack for the embalming fluid, were still in the basement. All this made the place spooky and no one stayed there for long. In one of the upper rooms was a child's casket – empty, thank goodness. This is probably the reason that the Western Hotel is now known for its ghosts and spirits. There have been so many appearances that the hotel even has a book in which their guests can record their experiences with ghosts or the paranormal. All of the experiences have been spooky but not dangerous.

A Western Hotel contractor in 1976 stated that his tools were being moved every night and that he saw shadows on the walls. After the hotel was occupied again it was almost immediately reported that it contained ghosts. There have also been paranormal events in the

Ouray Courthouse late at night such as doors rattling like someone is trying to get in and lights dimming and coming back on. A paranormal research team even spent the night there but did not record any unusual sights or sounds.

The Western Hotel, nick named "The Miner's Palace" was used for the wake of many deceased miners – one of which is seen here.

(Author's Collection)

THE UTE LEGEND AT BEAR CREEK FALLS
Many Tears Still Fall

Many drivers heading south from Ouray on Highway 550 toward Silverton stop a couple of miles south at the Bear Creek Falls Overlook, to get out and experience a large 227 foot waterfall as seen from the top. It is a dramatic view and at certain times there will be a rainbow in the falls. However only a few take in the view across the Uncompahgre River to the other side of the canyon, where there is a cliff that has strange ripples that look like water had formed them on a beach, but the formation usually only has water, if at all, for a short time during the spring runoff or after heavy rains. Some locals call this the "Wall of Tears" or more scientifically "The Trachtye Wall" but seeing it as a formation formed by tears running down it. Next to it is a small creek that usually has another pretty waterfall, but also sometimes becomes dry.

There is a Ute legend that a great Native American battle took place below this spot. The battle began in the Ouray bowl, but the Ute warriors were eventually driven south along the Uncompahgre River to this spot on the river, where they could retreat no more and were slaughtered there by the other Indian tribe. The formation across the creek was supposedly formed by their women and children, who had followed from safety at the top of the cliffs along the river to watch the battle below and who cried their tears so heavily that the formation was formed. This is the story as heard several times by the author from different people.

There is a slightly different version of this tale told by Roger Henn in his book *Lies, Legends and Lore*, in which he reports that some call the falls "Bridal Veil," some call it "mare's tail," and some call it "Indian Tears" after the Ute legend. Henn notes that Ouray's bowl may have been especially sacred to the Utes because of its medicinal hot springs. One day the spot was found by another tribe but the Utes soon drove them away. The intruding Indians were forced south alongside the Uncompahgre River and it was their women and children who ended up watching from the other side of the canyon. The intruding warriors all fought to their death. Supposedly the Utes named the waterfall "Indian Tears." Henn writes that this story was related to one of the first settlers of Ouray by an ancient Ute who passed through the town.

The Trachtye Wall or "Wall of Tears" (left at bottom) as used as one of the illustrations in blind poet Alfred King's books. He wrote it was "a symbol of eternal strength." (Author's Collection)

THE UTE CURSE ON THE UNCOMPAHGRE VALLEY
They Certainly Had Reason to Curse

The Tabeguache were the largest subgroup of the Ute Indians and were eventually headed by Chief Ouray, who the U. S. Government called on at times to represent the seven Ute bands of Colorado during the early 1860s to early 1880s. Chief Ouray and the Utes were successful in holding on to all of their traditional land until 1868, but in that year they gave up title to all the land east of the Continental Divide in most of Colorado. In large part they gave up the eastern half of today's Colorado because that land was already controlled by Americans. By giving up what they no longer controlled, the Utes hoped that the Americans would honor the land designated as being theirs under the treaty. Whites were allowed to have roads and travel through Ute territory, but they could not live there.

It took only four years before the Whites were back asking the Utes to sell them the San Juan Mountains, as rich deposits of silver and some gold had been discovered there. The Utes were at first very hesitant as they had been promised they would own this land "forever," but the San Juan Mountains were of marginal use to the Utes, who were nomadic hunters, and little game or edible food was found high in the mountains where the miners and prospectors would be. Eventually the Utes agreed to sell the San Juans and the prospectors moved into the mountains in 1874, but it was still decades before the Utes received most of their money for the sale.

Then in 1879 the northern Colorado Utes rebelled at the Meeker Agency and killed Meeker and all the male Americans employees there. Agent Meeker had been determined to make farmers out the Utes under his control, an action they were utterly adverse to. The Utes had lived their nomadic life in Colorado for hundreds of years, living relatively well off the land without having to do American work such as farming and ranching. The Southern Utes (Mouache, Capote, and

Weeminuch) had already been given reservations in southern Colorado and they refused to be moved. The northern Utes realized they
would have to give up their traditional land and left for Utah. This left
the Tabeguache in central Colorado. They had not participated in the
Meeker massacre, and had actually saved the American women and
children from the Meeker Agency and managed to keep the other Ute
tribes from starting a massive war that would have meant the annihila-
tion of the entire Ute tribe as well as hundreds or thousands of Whites.

Treaty talks were started yet again and the Tabeguache were initially to have been given land along the Gunnison and Uncompahgre
Rivers and around Grand Mesa. When the treaty was actually made,
two events changed the American position. The first was that Chief
Ouray died and there seemed to be no successor to deal with all the
Ute tribes. The second was that the actual treaty contained a provision
that if the land around the Grand Valley and Grand Mesa was not
useable for agriculture, the Tabeguache Utes could be moved to a reservation in Utah. Somehow it was found that there was no such usable
land in Colorado, and the Utes should be moved to the reservation in
Utah. When they protested, they were eventually moved by force by
the U.S. Army to a place appropriately called "Bitter Creek" on what is
called the "Ouray Ute Reservation." The Utes certainly had reason to
curse the Americans at this time, but some say their "witch doctors" or
medicine men put a curse specifically on the Uncompahgre and Grand
Valleys. This curse has been written up several times by American jour-
nalists, but there really is no evidence that anything happened because
of such a curse (if it ever existed).

Various statements of the actual terms of the curse include:

> *Nothing would grow and no one would ever be successful (this was
> the originally printed curse).*

> *No one would ever want to live on this cursed land.*

> *Once you left the area you would be destined to return at some later
> time.*

> *If you take dirt or a rock from the Valley when you left you will
> never return.*

And there are many other versions.

Research and discussions with various Ute elders have led Ute experts to the conclusion that no such curse exists or ever existed, yet the legend persists. What was called "Black Sunday" when oil shale was abandoned in Western Colorado has been pointed to as a result of the curse. Over the years almost anything negative that happens is often blamed on the curse, even marriages that have gone bad. By the way, the same curse has been said to have been placed just about anywhere that Whites are now living on what was Native American land. Of course lots of bad things have happened over the years. Should we blame them all on the Utes or ourselves?

The Tabeguache Utes leave Colorado for their new reservation in Utah. They cross the Colorado River near today's Grand Junction which was supposed to have been where they would be relocated.

(Author's Collection)

FURTHER READING

If you are interested in further reading, there are many full length books that cover many of the stories described in this book.

A Quick History of Ouray by P. David Smith

In the San Juans by Reverend J. J. Gibbons

The Irrepressible David F. Day by Duane Smith

The Handclasp of the East and West by Henry Ripley

The Life of the Marlows Edited by Judge William Rathnell

Father Struck It Rich by Evalyn Walsh McClean

A History of Ouray (2 Volumes) by Doris Gregory

The Road That Silver Built (Million Dollar Highway) by P. David Smith

Mountains of Silver (Red Mountain Mining District) by P. David Smith

Exploring the San Juan Triangle by P. David Smith

Silver and Sawdust by Roger Henn

Ouray by Jack Benham

Of Record and Reminisce by Ruth Rathnell

Images of the San Juans by P. David Smith

Ouray Chief of the Utes by P. David Smith

Chipeta Queen of the Utes by Cynthia Becker and P. David Smith

Pioneering in the San Juan by Reverend George Darley

One Man's West by David Lavendar